Marketing Planning for Financial Services

To Edith May Stephenson
1905–1988

Marketing Planning for Financial Services

ROY STEPHENSON

GOWER

Published by
Gower Publishing Limited
Gower House
Croft Road
Aldershot
Hants GU11 3HR
England

Gower Publishing Company
Suite 420
101 Cherry Street
Burlington,
VT 05401-4405
USA

Roy Stephenson has asserted his right under the Copyright, Designs and Patents Act 1988 to be identified as the author of this work.

British Library Cataloguing in Publication Data
Stephenson, Roy
    Marketing planning for financial services
    I. Financial services - Marketing
    I. Title
    322.1'0688

Library of Congress Control Number: 2004110142

ISBN 0 566 08554 2

Typeset by Bournemouth Colour Press, Parkstone, Poole.
Printed in Great Brtain by MPG Books Ltd, Bodmin.

Contents

Preface

The financial services industry is one of the most rapidly growing in the world economy: 50 years ago, financial services accounted for less than 3 per cent of GDP in developed Europe and the US; today, that number is approaching 10 per cent (*Independent/Merrill Lynch*, 23 January 2004). But despite its size and the national and even global reach of its biggest members, the marketing function surprisingly often is not handled by specialists: too frequently, managers' career progressions include a couple of years in marketing sandwiched in between other assignments. Large banks are particularly guilty in this regard. The result is that not enough executives have the time or motivation ever to become really familiar with the tools of the trade, let alone to build up the experience which can help decision-making when, as often, there is insufficient data to point to a clear choice of action.

Accordingly, my aim has been to help managers who have been newly appointed to marketing positions in the financial services industry by presenting the basic marketing planning concepts. I have not tried to describe them in detail: there are any number of excellent text books dealing with the ideas which are only outlined here. Rather, my objective has been to show what these methods are capable of and, by setting them specifically in the context of the industry, the hope is that this book will provide a highly relevant introduction to them. It also aims to be practical: it draws on a lifetime's experience, both as a practising manager and as an independent consultant to the industry. By reflecting experience gained around the world, it also hopes to be as useful to managers in developing economies as it is to their colleagues who can rely on efficient postal services, sophisticated credit bureaux and industrial-strength data management capabilities.

The examples given are very often taken from the payments card sector. Partly, this reflects my own background; much more important is that this is almost certainly the most advanced part of the financial services industry in its use of marketing techniques. What card marketers are doing today, investment product marketers will probably be doing tomorrow.

Any book has to have some kind of formal organisation. This one is structured around the steps which would be involved in launching and subsequently managing a new product, simply because this approach seemed to provide a logical framework and to include most of the techniques and ways of thinking that I wanted to describe. The individual chapters are intended broadly to reflect the individual phases of that process. It is only fair to warn, however, that this is an attempt to impose order on reality, and the real world is a good deal less compartmentalised than the chapter headings would suggest: pricing cannot be thought of in isolation from positioning or distribution, for example. Also, although the phased approach I propose is one which has worked well in practice, I make no claim that it is the only solution.

Readers may wonder why a book dealing with marketing planning lays so much emphasis on issues other than marketing. There are two practical reasons: firstly, responsibility for implementing the entire launch project is quite often placed with the marketing group. In this case, the product champion will need to co-ordinate the activities of all the other units which will be involved. Secondly, I believe that marketers should be able to see the business in the round: the organisation's progress and their personal development will both benefit if they understand at least the basics of finance and operations.

For those who are already hard-bitten practitioners, most of the material covered will already be familiar. However, the book may perhaps be helpful as a bringing together of everything they know and do successfully every day; at best, I hope that they may find one or two new insights.

Acknowledgements

I have had the great good fortune to work with outstanding teachers and colleagues: a hopelessly incomplete list would include G. H. Northing, Professor Gilbert Walker, Aubrey Morris, Sid Silver, Julian Waterman, Andy Sawicki, Peter Finch, Alan Kennedy, Nigel Ellis, Lenny Koven, Tommaso Zanzotto, Roger Ballou, Roger Hymas, Alex Bennigsen, Martin Leggett, Frank Kelly, Alan Deller, Keith Mills, Liam Cowdrey, Philip Beard, Ron Mazursky, Tony Clarke and the outstanding people at MasterCard Advisors. It gives me real pleasure to acknowledge my debt to all of them.

CHAPTER 1

Getting Started

STRUCTURE AND ASSUMPTIONS

There is no obviously best way of organising the material which this book covers. In the event, I have chosen to use a new product launch as the structure. The reasons for this approach are:

- It best illustrates the whole range of marketing techniques to be used.

- It emphasises that there is a logical process of thought and execution (this helps ensure a comprehensive and orderly approach, rather than the 'Ready Fire Aim' method).

- Effectively the same techniques are also used in relaunch, although the sequence of actions and the underlying thinking are likely to be a little different.

To provide a complete overview of marketing activity, the final chapter examines the issues involved in product management once the product has been brought to market.

Product launch, or any other marketing task, tends to present itself as a series of questions to be answered: 'What is the product?', 'Who is going to buy it?', 'What price should we sell it at?' and so on. To the first-timer, the number of questions seems to be matched only by their interdependence: to answer any one, it can seem that all the others need to be resolved.

But there is a sequential way of thinking about the questions, and therefore of organising the task. The structure of the text suggests a systematic approach to the project, by breaking it up into sections, such as 'product definition', 'market definition', and so on. Within each of these, the text suggests what questions the manager needs to answer, and then proposes ways of answering them.

One final point: throughout, the book assumes that the business context is that of a commercial organisation, and that the main success criterion will usually therefore be whether the product makes a profit generating an adequate return on resources invested. This will not always be the case: a mutually owned organisation, for example, may not seek to maximise profit. Equally, on the loss-leader principle, a business may continue to market a product which at best breaks even because providing it is a prerequisite for selling other, more profitable, services: an example would be a stockbroker's securities research department.

Nevertheless, the book's approach will still generally be valid: it will simply be necessary to substitute for profit whatever other measure the organisation uses to allocate resource and measure success.

GETTING ORGANISED

Virtually all product launches begin from one of three positions:

- We have developed a new product.

- There appears to be a gap in the market.

- There is a gap in our product range.

Reasons to Launch a New Product

We have developed a new product

In response to UK Government regulations requiring the introduction of low cost so-called 'stakeholder' pensions/ISAs.

There appears to be a gap in the market

For an annuity product which has a residual value for the beneficiaries of holders who die before an agreed term of years.

There is a gap in our product range

For a payment card designed to meet the needs of small businesses.

Whichever of these applies in our case (and there may be more than one), we will be faced with answering the same questions:

- What is the product?

- How will it be produced and distributed?

- What will it cost to produce and bring to market?

- Who is likely to buy it?

- What is the competition?

- Are there any laws or other regulations which affect it?

- Do we have enough resources internally to produce, distribute, market and manage it?

- If not, where will we find them, and on what terms?

- Will it be profitable?

- How will we get internal approval to develop the product?

- How should we plan development and launch?

- How will we communicate the product to the market?

- How do we manage the product to maximise profitability once it has been launched?

Each question does not necessarily have to be answered in precisely this order: for example, it would be just as reasonable to ask 'Who is likely to buy it?' immediately after 'What is the product?' But overall the flow reflects the sequence in which the plan's components usually come together.

There is a further issue which needs to be considered when mapping out the project plan: who needs to know the answers, and why? In other words, to whom am I going to present the results of my work, and what do I expect to happen as a result?

New products have to compete with a huge variety of other projects jostling for scarce funds – scarce, that is, in the economist's sense, that there are fewer funds than claims upon them. In many organisations, these investment planning decisions are seen as one of senior management's most important tasks, and a formal process has been built to deal with them.

The process will vary from business to business but one frequently found approach is to set the project up in a series of phases, perhaps along the lines set out in Figure 1.1. The advantage of this method is that it quickly filters out those projects which fail the criteria for that phase, and therefore avoids wasting time and money. It may be thought of building a sequential series of hypotheses, each of which has to be tested, the data becoming successively more complete and the criteria more rigorous at each stage.

SUMMING UP

The first task to face anyone starting a complex project is to organise it in some way which makes it approachable and manageable. One possibility is to adopt a structure which follows an orderly sequence. This book uses the challenge of a new product launch as a way of organising the material to be covered.

With this in mind, it then becomes possible to arrange the very many questions which need answering into a sequence which makes sense. For instance, tempting though it may be to start considering the creative aspects of the launch campaign straight away, it will almost certainly be necessary first to define the product, the target market, production strategy, distribution channels, delivery systems, pricing and many other issues.

It is also possible to use this sequential approach to set up the assignment in a series of phases which will facilitate the decision-making process without wasting time or money on projects which do not meet pre-established criteria.

Phase I: Preliminary Survey

This work will probably be based on desk research, without incurring the expense of internal or external studies. Its purpose is simply to explore whether there is sufficient evidence to warrant undertaking a feasibility study.

Phase II: Feasibility Study

This seeks to confirm the findings of the preliminary survey by much more detailed work, probably including consumer research and internal studies. It will aim to set business criteria which, if met, will give management authorisation to create a business plan.

Phase III: Business Plan

Building on the findings of the feasibility study, this phase will see the development, probably by a dedicated team, of a business plan, covering all of the issues involved in business launch and management. Approval of the plan will trigger resource commitment and launch.

Phase IV: Launch

Phase IV calls for the execution of the launch plan on the lines agreed. Crucially, from a financial point of view, it is likely to see major expenditures without corresponding revenues.

Phase V: Product Management

The product is now launched: the focus therefore changes to how best to secure profitable growth. This requires techniques significantly different from those involved in bringing the product to market.

Figure 1.1 A phased approach to product marketing

Hypothesis Testing
Launching a loyalty programme in the Netherlands

Building on the success of the Air Miles programme in the UK, LMI, the company which had developed the concept, identified the Netherlands as a potential market in which to launch a similar programme. Working with partners in banking, the airline industry, supermarkets and retail, LMI took on the responsibility of examining the commercial viability of such a scheme. To do this, it established a working group with representatives from each of the major partners. The group was tasked with answering a series of questions:

Phase I: Preliminary survey

Are there sufficient market similarities between the Netherlands and the UK for there to be a prima facie *case for launching a programme?*

Most of the material was readily available from desk research – population size, age profile, retail infrastructure, travel habits, use of banking products, buying habits, experience with brand promotional activity.

Answer:
Yes, the market is smaller, but in all other ways there are considerable similarities. Furthermore, Dutch consumers have long been enthusiastic savers in a promotional scheme run by a leading coffee brand.

Phase II: Feasibility study

How big would the market be? Would the scheme be legal? How would members be enrolled? What would be the tax implications for savers and issuers of points? How would points be awarded and credited to savers' accounts? Would it be possible to set up a call centre to answer requests for information and award redemptions? What would be the systems requirements? How would the scheme be structured so as to be attractive to collectors while affordably creating the changes in buying preferences sought by the partners?

Answer:
In general terms, the responses to all these questions are positive. With some out-sourcing, it could be done.

Phase III: Business plan

What would it take to launch the business, and would these requirements, and the consequent outcomes, meet agreed criteria?

Answer:
The requirement here was for the group to develop specific and detailed plans with goals and timings under the headings of:

- Marketing
- Business operations
- Systems
- Finance
- Human resources
- Legal

In practice, it was found easiest for specialist working groups to be set up to handle each of these themes; continuity was achieved by the overall working group which provided a permanent secretariat and was responsible for co-ordinating each specialist group's contributions into an integrated plan.

On the basis of this plan, it was possible to generate sales forecasts, systems requirements, staffing levels, a profit and loss account, cash flow statement, balance sheet and impact statements for each of the partners' businesses. These met the business requirements which had previously been established and the management committee was therefore able to give the project the go-ahead to plan for launch.

CHAPTER 2

Defining the Product

INTRODUCTION

To move a product from being what appears to be an interesting idea to one which is capable of commanding substantial investment resources and generating large sales revenues, rigorous thinking is required. First, it will be necessary to ask some very fundamental questions about what the product does. More broadly, we will also need to consider the product in its commercial context – how it is to be priced, produced, serviced and marketed. Accordingly, this process will also require a preliminary consideration of topics which subsequently will be explored in much more detail. Though the questions posed are simple enough to express, responding to them will require careful thought.

WHAT ARE THE ISSUES?

The first steps in launching a new product are deciding precisely what the product is to be, who might buy it, how we are to communicate it to potential customers, how it will be produced and put into customers' hands, and what price it could be sold at. Above all, we need to ask ourselves what our brainchild will do better than products which are already on offer in the market place.

Spelling out these issues in rather more detail, we arrive at the following series of questions:

Product content

- What does it do (sometimes known as the consumer proposition, or value proposition)?

- How does it do it?

- Is it the same across all market segments? (Better-off, home-owners, young family, retired, students, sub-prime, savers, ethnic minorities, small companies, farmers…)

- If not, what segmentation structure is proposed? (For example, tiering, menu of choices, risk-based pricing, niche marketing…)

Product positioning

- What will be the product's most important characteristic from the user's point of view: convenience, price, lifestyle…?

- Will it be a stand-alone product, or will it fit into an existing range of products?

Product sourcing and delivery

- Will we be able to produce it using only our own internal resources?
- If not, who will be our partners in production?

Product distribution

- Will we be able to distribute it using only our own internal resources?
- If not, who will be our partners in distribution?

Price

- How much will it cost to produce and get to market?
- How does this compare with similar products already in the market place, if any?

Competitive advantage

- What does this product do better than the competition?

In the case of EasyLoan, it seems likely that the most important customer benefit is the speed with which the application can be processed. (In this context, note that according to a report from the New York based Information Policy Institute, prior to automated underwriting, approving a mortgage loan in the US took nearly three weeks on average. In 2002, more than 75 per cent of all loan applications received approval in two to three minutes (*CardFlash* 18 June 2003).) The other key benefit is the competitive interest rate.

The question then arises, which consumer group is most likely to react favourably to this combination of features? The answer to this will in its turn help define the communication media and distribution channels to be used. Clearly, response times measured in minutes are most effective when delivered electronically, so on the face of it, EasyLoan is likely to do best among customers who are connected to the Internet and/or have bought goods or services by phone in the past. Apart from any internal records which we may have of existing customers who meet these criteria, it is possible to buy lists of both these groups.

It may be evident from this more complex example that one of the benefits of this approach is that it compels us to think more clearly and precisely about the product to be marketed. Already, for instance, we have had to think about who the user will be, and it seems that in this case there will be two sets of users: the traveller, and a financial manager. Not only will there be two sets of users, each set will be looking for quite distinct benefits. In fact, in this particular case, to some extent the benefits are in conflict: the traveller out on the road will want the flexibility of being able to use the

---

DEFINING THE PRODUCT 1

The Acme Capital EasyLoan

Product content

- *What does it do?*
  Acme Capital's EasyLoan product offers creditworthy customers fast decisions and competitive rates on secured loans up to £25 000.

- *How does it do it?*
  By electronically accessing credit agencies' automated consumer records, Acme Capital's credit scoring software provides decisioning capability within an average of 30 seconds. Accordingly, phone and Internet applicants can have a loan decision almost immediately.

- *Is it the same across all market segments?*
  EasyLoan will be available to all creditworthy applicants with sufficient home equity to secure the loan.

- *If not, what segmentation structure is proposed?*
  Although the product will be the same, lower rates will be offered for larger loans.

Product positioning

- *What will be the product's most important characteristic from the user's point of view?*
  Speed and simplicity.

- *Will it be a stand-alone product, or will it fit into an existing range of products?*
  EasyLoan will fill a gap in our existing portfolio of credit products, between car loans and mortgages.

Product sourcing and delivery

- *Will we be able to produce it using only our own internal resources?*
  No. For decisioning capability, we will rely on proprietary scoring software evaluating credit bureau data. Phone application traffic volumes can be handled using existing under-utilised call centre capacity, but the website will need to be modified to include the new product. Funding needs can be met using established in-house lines of credit.

Product distribution

- *Will we be able to distribute it using only our own internal resources?*
  Yes. To keep costs low, we will not be marketing EasyLoan through third parties.

Price

- *How much will it cost to produce and get to market? How does this compare with similar products already in the market place, if any?*
  Preliminary cost analysis shows we should be able to beat the price of competitive offerings from other banks.

Competitive advantage

- *What does this product do better than the competition?*
  Compared with traditional, paper-based lenders, EasyLoan provides very much faster decisions. Compared with the new web-based lenders, we are much better known.

---

card in as many types of establishment as possible, whereas the financial manager may prefer to restrict the range of merchants who can accept the card. This tension between flexibility and control could well affect how we communicate the product's benefits: perhaps we will have to devise two types of message and maybe even think about choosing different media to reach these different audiences. The product positioning will also probably have to be somewhat different for the two groups.

DEFINING THE PRODUCT 2

The Acme Bank Corporate Card

Product content
- *What does it do?*
  Acme Bank's proposed Corporate Card allows companies to control their travel and entertainment expenditures more closely, while providing travellers with a means of charging their expenses while they are away from the office.

- *How does it do it?*
  The plastic card provides the charging method. Software analyses transactions to provide budgetting control and analysis in either standard format reports, or reports tailored to customers' specific needs.

- *Is it the same across all market segments?*
  Targeted at all companies employing more than 250 staff.

- *If not, what segmentation structure is proposed?*
  An optional Gold version with enhanced benefits will be offered for senior managers.

Product positioning
- *What will be the product's most important characteristic from the user's point of view?*
  For the traveller: convenience and security. For management: reduced administration and better control of expenses.

- *Will it be a stand-alone product, or will it fit into an existing range of products?*
  It will be the first of a range of card-based corporate payment solutions, to include small business and purchasing cards.

Product sourcing and delivery
- *Will we be able to produce it using only our own internal resources?*
  Yes. Systems, Finance and Operations confirm in-house capability.

Product distribution
- *Will we be able to distribute it using only our own internal resources?*
  Yes, using branch network and corporate relationship team.

Price
- *How much will it cost to produce and get to market? How does this compare with similar products already in the market place, if any?*
  Preliminary cost analysis shows we should be able to beat or match the price of competitive offerings.

Competitive advantage
- *What does this product do better than the competition?*
  Compared with the market leader it is at parity in terms of management information system, but significantly better in terms of the numbers of outlets which accept the card.

We may also have to think a little more carefully about who this 'financial manager' might be: will it be the finance director, or someone lower down in the hierarchy? Very likely their needs will be different. For example, the finance director is likely to be concerned with overall cost reduction and improvements in cash flow, whereas managers a couple of levels down may simply be looking for ways to cut paperwork and make it easier to check staff expense claims. Nor should we fall into the trap of assuming that because managers are at a lower level, they have no say in the purchase decision: they can often be important influencers.

Not only will user needs be different, the channels for reaching them are also likely to be different: road warriors may not share the finance director's taste for *The Economist* and the *Financial Times*. Naturally, there will be overlaps: it is unrealistic to assume that no one will see both messages. Accordingly, it would be important to ensure that there is no inherent conflict in the positioning.

Rigorous thinking about what the product does must also include an honest assessment of what it does better than current offerings. In the financial services industry, the costs of developing and launching a new product are often very low, certainly by comparison with the investments required in other industries (consider the billions of pounds it costs to design a new aero-engine, for example). As a consequence, all too many products in the sector are launched simply because the competition is doing them, or because 'We are a financial supermarket, and we need a presence in every sector'. Very little effort is ever given in these cases to determining whether these products are actually earning their keep by generating real profit (and I shall have more to say about that later) or bringing in profitable new customers who otherwise we would not reach, or keeping existing profitable customers who otherwise might go elsewhere. One undesirable outcome is that the sales effort is blunted because the people responsible have too many products to sell. Generally, an understandable pride of ownership should not be allowed to generate overly favourable opinions of a product's true competitive strength.

PRODUCT RESEARCH

Surveys are often mounted to explore market attitudes to an existing product or service; properly designed, research of this sort should yield valuable information.

However, where research is used to examine reactions to, or suggestions for, a product which does not yet exist, it is as well to be cautious in developing the survey and interpreting the results. Customers' ability to indicate whether they would use something outside their experience is limited: who would have predicted that in some European markets mobile phone penetration would reach 75 per cent? (Nick Jones, Gartner Group, *Business in a Wireless World*, CBI/IBM) Nor is the good technology/bad technology yardstick a useful guide: SMS text messaging is slow, cumbersome, fiddly – and immensely successful with customers, because it is cheap and delivers something they find very useful. WAP-enabled banking, on the other hand, has been a failure: that it exists at all is a major engineering achievement – but customers find it gives them very little added value. One solution is to ask customers questions about what outcomes they want (fixed outgoings, for example) rather than the products or processes which might deliver them.

SUMMING UP

This stage may be thought of as a first attempt to see the product clearly, and in its business setting. Its purpose is to provide preliminary definitions, identify potential opportunities, and point to possible weaknesses which need to be addressed. Not only is this approach valuable in itself, it also provides the platform for answering questions and making decisions which come later in the process.

CHAPTER 3

Defining the Customer

INTRODUCTION

Hand in hand with the question 'What is the product?' goes its companion 'Who is likely to buy it?' In order to market a product successfully, we must have a clear idea about its potential customers:

- to be able to identify the communication media which will reach them most cost-effectively (specialist investment magazines, the tabloid press, ads on Internet portals, direct mail, statement inserts...);

- to know how they are likely to use the product (buying a rental property, paying for school fees, pension provision...);

- to understand their attitudes to the product (grudging, puzzled, optimistic) and its providers (positive, suspicious, pragmatic...).

Knowing the answers to these questions will improve our ability to design the product, choose media and frame the message we want to communicate about the product.

MARKET SEGMENTATION

So how do we set about defining the customer? Or, putting the question another way, which segments of the total market will find it most attractive and relevant to their needs? The process of market segmentation is essentially about finding labels to describe the potential customer – but it is essential that the labels be usable. Knowing that our new service will appeal strongly to people with red hair is not very helpful if we do not know how to reach them.

Possible labels – or segmentation categories – are to do with:

1. what the product's potential customers look like (demographics);

2. how they behave (good credit risks, regular savers, Internet users...);

3. what their attitudes are (cautious investors, free spenders, environmentally concerned...).

Their value for two important communications functions varies – see Figure 3.1.

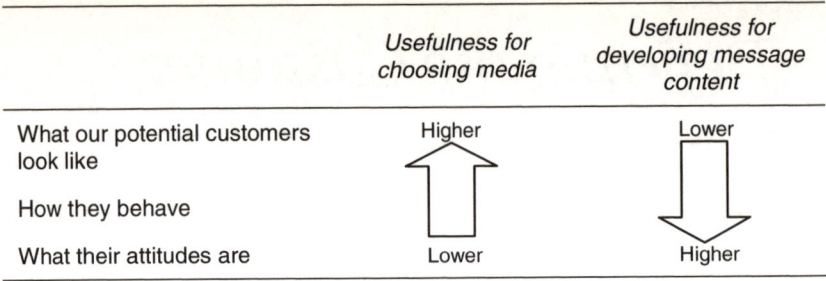

	Usefulness for choosing media	*Usefulness for developing message content*
What our potential customers look like	Higher	Lower
How they behave		
What their attitudes are	Lower	Higher

Figure 3.1 The value of customer descriptions for two important communications functions

Studies designed to answer questions about customer description usually come under the heading of qualitative research.

The Power of Market Segmentation

When I was working as a holiday representative in Mallorca, one of my main functions was to sell excursions, on which I earned a commission. At that time, the 'official' range ran to nine excursions, some of which were only doubtfully attractive, while others were big sellers. Describing all of these at the obligatory Welcome Party was a chore for all concerned, and produced only modest sales. To make life easier for everybody, I dropped most of them, and concentrated on two night life excursions and two scenic trips. Sales grew, and the Welcome Parties were a lot less tedious. The breakthrough came when I recognised that what suited teenagers was anathema to the elderly. Accordingly, I packaged them into the 'FunLovers' Special', and the 'Island Explorer', with discounts on the price of the individual trips. I earned more money, clients were better served, and we all got to the beach much faster.

In market segmentation, the main task of qualitative research is dealing with 'Who are our customers? What do they look like? Where can we find them?' Clearly, these questions are also closely linked to the issue of 'How many of them are there?' In other words, 'How big is the market?', which is the subject of the next chapter. But it is worth noting that the boundaries between qualitative (Who, What, How and Why?) and quantitative research (How many?) are not always clear-cut, and that intelligently used qualitative research can help provide answers to quantitative-type questions.

Assuming, for the sake of simplicity, that we are dealing with a product which is already on the market, then our task becomes one of finding existing users, deciding what characteristics they have in common, and then trying to identify clusters of consumers who, because they have a similar profile, are therefore also potential users.

If we already have customers for a similar product, then it is simply a question of surveying them. If we do not currently offer the product, then finding existing users of financial services is very much helped by the existence of a number of databases, commercially managed and constantly updated, which provide access to statistically valid groups of customers for virtually any major product or service. As just one example, Experian in the US holds data on 215 million consumers in 110 million households, 330 million vehicles, 40 million homeowners and 15 million businesses. It also claims to have self-reported information on 30 million consumers, and access to more than 100 million permission-based e-mail addresses.

Such databases usually allow analysis by:

Demographics

Gender

Age

Occupation

Marital status

Address

Number of children

Educational qualifications

Sociographics

Newspapers read regularly

TV viewing habits

Holidays taken

Type of home

Cars in household

Financial products owned

Current account

Mortgage

Savings products

Securities

Pensions

Loans

Card products

Insurance

Lifestage

Young single

DINKs (double income, no kids)

Newly–weds

Young family

School age children

Empty nesters…

Long as it is, this listing by no means exhausts the customer data which is available; but not all of these characteristics will be relevant for the purpose of segmenting the market. For the moment, it will probably be enough to collect sufficient information about the current base of customers to be able to profile them with reasonable accuracy.

A wide variety of statistical tools is available to analyse the data in order to understand which of the virtually infinite range of variables are good predictors of behaviour. Perhaps the most common of the many multivariate techniques is cluster analysis, but financial services companies are making increasing use of neural networks, which identify complex patterns within a database to make forecasts about outcomes associated with those patterns. (The technique is also used to highlight potentially fraudulent transactions.)

Accordingly, following analysis, we might conclude that the typical first-time buyer of medical insurance is a home-owner, male, married with children, with an annual income of at least £30 000 and aged between 30 and 40. If we aim to market the product to our existing customers, then it will be necessary to search the client database to identify individuals who fit this profile. (This, incidentally, underlines the value of collecting as much customer data as possible – both when they are recruited, and during customer service conversations.) If we are also targeting prospects who currently are not doing business with us, we have seen that research companies maintain up to date and highly detailed databases covering virtually every conceivable segmentation variable.

Applying this profile to the population as a whole may reveal that there are, say, 4.5 million individuals like this in the UK market. This gives the consumer dimension to our market size question, and multiplying this number by the typical policy premium provides an estimate of the market's annual value.

This process also helps to deal with 'Where can we find them?': media buyers can use profiling information to draw up a list of the media to which our potential customer is most frequently exposed, and which therefore will be the most effective way of reaching him.

Thus far, we have gone a very long way to answering the questions 'What does the potential customer look like?' and 'Where can we find him?' We may also have some answers to the question 'How does he behave?': it could well be that the data analysis of existing customers has turned up valuable information about other products held (mortgages and savings accounts, for example, the average balances and how long they have been open – tenure, as it is often called).

Essentially, we are trying to move along an axis from mass marketing to one-on-one marketing: the first approach assumes that all customers are the same, and have the same needs; the second works on the premise that all customers are individuals and that our marketing will be more effective if we offer them products that they (or people very like them) actually need. What makes the difference is data (see Figure 3.2 for example).

In payment card markets in the UK and Canada, respectively, LloydsTSB's Accucard and Bank of Montreal's Mosaik products have explored the one-on-one marketing concept by allowing customers virtually to create their own card, selecting

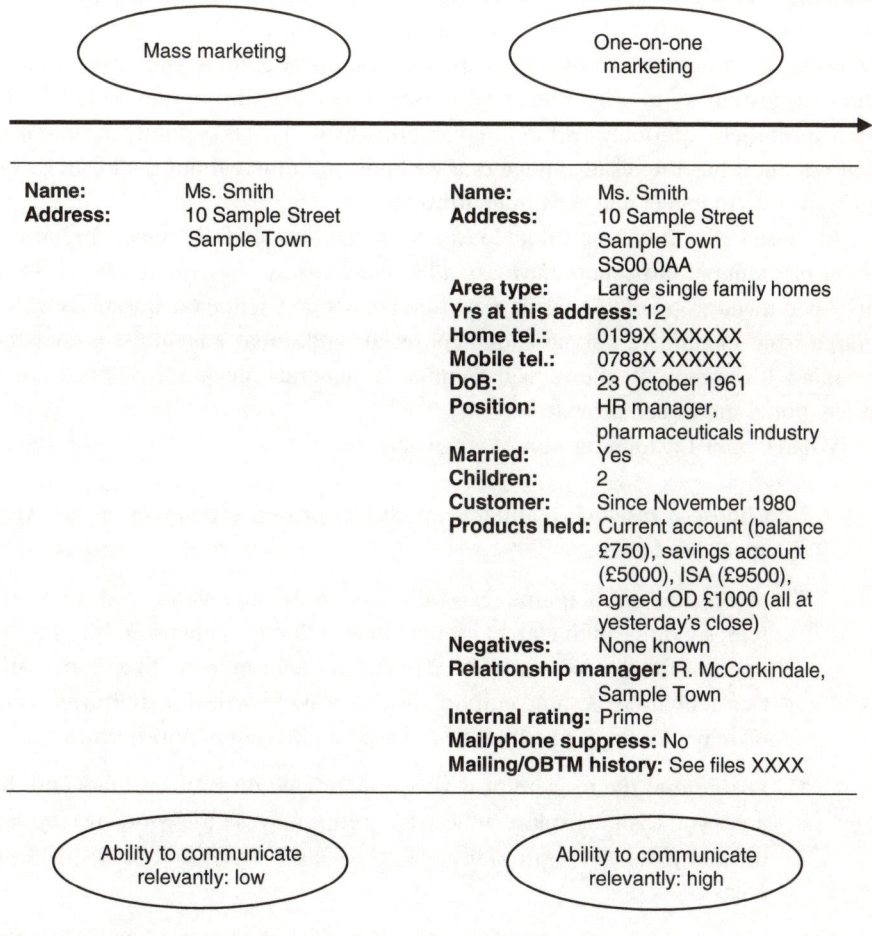

Figure 3.2 Using data to move to one-on-one marketing

the combination of APR, fee, card design and rewards programme which best meets their needs.

The area remaining to be investigated is 'What are the customer's attitudes? Why does the customer do this?' It is unlikely that answers to this will be found by examining databases: we will have to ask the client directly.

UNDERSTANDING CUSTOMER ATTITUDES

Because behaviour is strongly associated with the way people feel, understanding consumer attitudes is a key step to successful product development. In fact, attitudinal research is an important branch of qualitative research.

Here, we are dealing with questions rather less easy to answer than 'Do you have a life assurance policy?' Instead, our interest is in 'Why do you have (or not have) a life assurance policy?' The responses therefore will range much more broadly than Yes or No. But to get some kind of useful response to a question, as well as to make sure that important attitudes are consistently explored, the questionnaire will have to make some suggestion as to what those responses might be. One option would be to brainstorm them internally, within the marketing team. This is certainly the quickest method, but it has the disadvantage that we know too much about the business for our responses to reflect real consumer attitudes.

In these cases, it will be valuable to let a small but carefully selected group of actual or potential customers have a guided conversation to explore the issues of interest. A focus group of this sort is very useful in helping define the questions which a large-scale qualitative survey should pose; an additional advantage is that the extended discussion it allows will frequently generate deeper insights than a conventional survey can provide.

When organising focus groups, it is sensible to:

- Choose a research company which has proven experience in this very specialised area.

- Select the participants carefully, not only to ensure that they are representative of the target group, but also that they are unlikely to inhibit open discussion of attitudes. (For instance, in markets like France and Germany there is some cultural disapproval of borrowing; borrowers may be reluctant to discuss their need for credit in front of non-borrowers.)

- Ensure that the moderator is very fully briefed on your business and the areas you wish to explore, otherwise groups may get the wrong perception of what you need them to discuss, or time will be wasted in less relevant areas.

- Take the opportunity to view the groups while they are happening; the video tapes which are normally supplied after the event do not allow you to take action at the time to correct a misunderstanding, or to take advantage of an interesting insight (though you should interrupt proceedings by sending in messages for the moderator as little as possible).

- Be willing to modify the agenda based on experience from previous sessions.

Carefully planned and executed focus groups will generate a wealth of useful information about customer attitudes to the product, how they could use it, what they feel about our company and their views about the competition. This will help to shape the product and also to provide valuable insights into how messages about the product should be phrased – their tone of voice, for example, and the language which it is best to use.

Focus groups are good at deciding which attitudes or behaviours to examine; but large-scale studies are needed to establish how widespread they are.

When planning large-scale research, sample design and questionnaire development are key to getting the most out of what will be a significant investment of money and time. There is an extensive technical literature on this subject. For our current purposes, the most important factors to bear in mind are:

- Do we want to talk to actual or potential customers, or both? Of our institution or our competitors, or both?

- How do we define them, so that we can find them and communicate with them?

- What do we actually need to find out? Is what we are planning to find out actionable?

- Financial products are complex: will respondents understand the questions as they are currently phrased?

An all-too-frequent mistake is to assume that what is true in one country will be true in another: as the table in Figure 3.3 demonstrates, consumer attitudes on key questions can show wide variations.

MERGING 'WHO ARE THEY?' WITH 'HOW DO THEY BEHAVE?'

It is when these two dimensions are brought together that we gain the richest (richest because most useful) understanding of our actual and potential customers.

For instance, research in the UK has suggested that age, family status, family size and income are useful tools for predicting what type of banking service customers will prefer (see Figure 3.4).

	US	UK	Spain	France	Poland	Germany	Italy	Japan
Consumer credit as % of disposable income	23	23	15	12	10	6	5	n/a
'I don't really understand about pensions, annuities, etc.' (%)	36	32	37	51	n/a	22	47	50
'I trust my bank to be honest and fair.' (%)	71	58	44	10	n/a	46	33	n/a

Source: Intersec Research/*The Economist* and HenleyWorld 2003.

Figure 3.3 Attitudes vary from country to country

Type of service	Customer age	Family status	Children	Income
Traditional High Street bank	50–65	Pre-retirement	Empty nester	>£75 000
Building society	35–49 (18–24 age group under-represented)	Married couples	Growing families	>£30 000
Online bank	25–29 (sharp decline after 50)	Male, co-habiting or separated, comfortable with new technology, less need for face-to-face contact	Children 10 years old or younger	£30 000–£75 000
Credit card issuer	25–49	Co-habiting or divorced	Children 15 years old or younger	£13 500–£50 000
Supermarket bank	40–59	Married, home mortgaged or owned outright		£25 000–£100 000 (skew to higher income)

Source: Based on Acxiom, quoted in *Marketing Week*, 7 August 2003

Figure 3.4 Some suggested characteristics of bank customers by type of banking services used

It would be wrong to read too much into this kind of research finding: in Figure 3.4 for instance, High Street banks will have very many customers who do not fit the suggested profile at all. Rather, what is being proposed is that particular sets of characteristics are over-represented within these groups.

Furthermore, the results are a snapshot, describing the situation at a particular moment in time. It would be inappropriate to extrapolate, and say that today's online banking customer will, as he matures, move his business to a High Street branch: just as possible is that online banks will find ways of providing the reassurance and enhanced service standards which older, better-off customers feel they find at High Street banks. The chart in Figure 3.5 shows one such trajectory.

Nevertheless, even with riders and provisos, it is clear that, judiciously used, data of this sort is very valuable in helping define what our existing customers look like and and how they behave – and also where we might think about extending our reach.

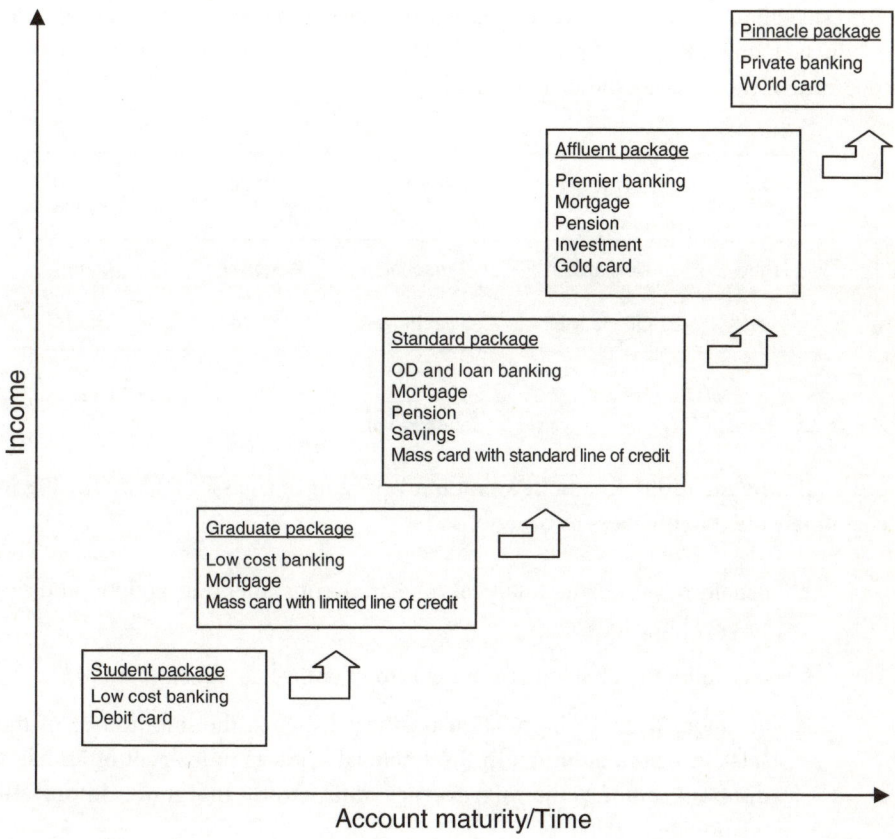

Figure 3.5 Possible product life cycle for personal banking. Who is the customer? Customers change over time

THE BUSINESS CUSTOMER

Perhaps inevitably, given the relative size of the promotional budgets involved, consumer marketing has more appeal to many practitioners than marketing to businesses. But business-to-business marketing – or B2B in the current phrase – has its own very real rewards: putting together a bid for a big contract, and then winning it against tough and capable competition is a very exciting experience. Furthermore, the financial services industry's biggest customers are businesses: it is important to understand how they make buying decisions.

This is not to say that all business marketing involves huge deals: a small builder buying public liability insurance is just as much a B2B transaction as a multinational deciding who should handle its next Eurobond offering. Very often, small business transactions can be handled in much the same way as consumer transactions: by mail, website or call centre, without the need to involve specialist selling staff. But the bigger the transaction, the greater the need for face-to-face communication, partly as a result of the greater value of the business on offer, and partly because there is a strong likelihood that at this level the service will need to be tailor-made in some way.

In fact, the value of the transaction will usually influence its position on a spectrum of variables, as shown in Figure 3.6.

Value	Product	Channel	Price	Time to arrange
Higher	Customised	Personal	Negotiated	Long
Lower	Off the shelf	Call centre/web	Fixed	Short

Figure 3.6 Effect of transaction value on selected variables

Generally, the main differences between marketing to businesses and marketing to consumers are that business transactions:

- usually have a higher financial value than consumer transactions, and can be very large indeed;

- take longer to conclude (months is frequent, years not unheard of);

- are more likely to be relationship-based (hence the importance of the sales function, although in the financial services industry it often has a different name); the bigger the transaction, the more important relationships will be;

- may involve a degree of customisation – again, the bigger the transaction, the more likely this will be – to adapt flexible product components to client needs;

- are likely to include a significant element of bargaining on price and service levels;

- may be on a test basis;

- could be implemented locally, nationally or around the world;

- may have many customers.

It is this last point which concerns us here. Business purchases will very often bring into play a variety of roles, as shown in Figure 3.7.

In very small businesses, these roles may all be carried out by one person: the owner/manager. But the bigger the organisation, the stronger the likelihood that the 'customer' will actually be many customers, very often sitting as a committee to agree the requirement, select potential vendors, issue a request for proposals to meet the need, evaluate the responses and finally decide which supplier gets the contract.

Role	Function	Possible criteria
The originator	The person who first identified the need for the product or service	More interested in 'What?' and 'How?' than 'How much?'. Can be a valuable ally
Influencers	Those whose views will be considered in making the decision. Some or all of: • Finance • Legal • HR • Senior management	Perspectives will vary according to their background: • Finance: 'Does this meet company financial requirements?' • Legal: 'How do I protect the company's interests?' • HR: 'Will this affect staff compensation and conditions?' • Senior management: 'What relations do we have this supplier (or its competitors)? Does this affect them?'
Decision maker	Probably a senior line manager	'Will it work? Does it improve my bottom line?'
Purchaser	Probably an individual in the purchasing department	'Are we getting the best possible deal? How do we set performance standards? How do we document this?'
Users	May be very many, may be geographically widely spread	'Will it make my life easier?'

Figure 3.7 Business purchases bring a variety of roles into play

Each of these customers will represent a particular constituency of interest, and therefore, not only must their biases and preferences as individuals be identified and catered for, the needs of the interest group which they represent must also be researched and responded to.

THE PUBLIC SECTOR AS CUSTOMER

Even after the long round of privatisation, nearly half the UK's domestic output is still created by the public sector – and the proportion is considerably higher in other countries. Accordingly, this is a customer which should be of greater interest to the financial services industry than sometimes it appears to be. It can be easy to underestimate just how far the sector extends: in the UK, as well as the archetypal Whitehall ministries, it includes the National Health Service, local government, most educational institutions, the armed forces, the emergency services, a glittering array of quangos and industry regulators, and much else besides.

Because ultimately its main source of income is the taxpayer, the public sector has to take greater care to be seen to be accountable than the private sector. It is also important to recognise that a much higher proportion of its staff are likely to be union members than is usually the case in the private sector: this will often mean taking account of arrangements which have been carefully negotiated over many years and which will not be easy to change. Again, the public sector is usually a primary vehicle for putting into effect formal and informal government policies about employment, the environment, financial standards, technology, and whatever else is of current concern. Another way in which the public and private sectors differ is that, because of its size and the undoubted credit of the government, the public sector frequently itself takes responsibility for functions which in the private sector would be contracted out; a commonly cited example is insurance. These characteristics influence the process of marketing to public bodies, usually in the direction of making the purchasing process longer, more detailed and more careful to ensure that all the entities who have any connection with the product or service are consulted.

Despite these variations from the norm, the public sector can be a very valuable customer for the financial services industry: the NHS, for instance, is the biggest employer in Europe, and has a correspondingly large requirement for products and services of all kinds.

SUMMING UP

It's crucial to have some understanding of what sort of customers are likely to buy the product, their attitudes to it, what use they will make of it, how they behave and make decisions, and at what stage they are in their lives. With this information, we can design the product better, understand how big the market could be, and make more informed choices about where and how to reach customers. Information of this sort can often be found in our own client databases. Commercial sources of information can either enrich internally held material or take its place if it is not available. Focus groups can help provide direction for larger-scale examinations of attitudes and behaviour. Whatever the context, research will be much more sharply targeted by bearing in mind the question: 'How will I use the data I expect to get from the study?'

Marketing does not stop with personal clients: the business sector is a major customer of the financial services industry. Selling products and services to commercial organisations requires an understanding of the much greater complexity of business-to-business decision-making. More specialised still is the public sector, but its sheer size makes it an attractive target for financial services marketers.

CHAPTER 4

Sizing the Market

INTRODUCTION

When launching a new product, most businesses will be concerned above all else by how profitable it is likely to be. This is not simply a matter of high margins: many financial service institutions are large organisations which are reluctant to have their product portfolios cluttered up with niche offerings which have no reasonable expectation of growth. Perhaps the most succinct expression of this view came from Jack Welch, former CEO of General Electric: he expected each of its many businesses to be number one or two in its field; if not, he closed or sold them. Business investment decisions almost always involve an opportunity cost – the income foregone by *not* investing in a different option – and his thinking clearly was that resources allocated to a product with limited potential could be better used in another which had the possibility of being a market leader.

An exception to this might be where a business unit serves some other purpose, such as being essential to serving a key consumer group which may well take more valuable business elsewhere if the niche product is not available. For instance, many banks have supported barely profitable shareholder registrar operations simply to provide a service to large corporate customers.

ESTIMATING THE VALUE OF THE MARKET

Accordingly, the question most usually asked of a product champion is 'How big is the market?' However, this contains within itself another question: 'What do we mean by market?', or as the statisticians would say, 'What is the universe?'

- Our existing customers?
- The country as a whole?
- A defined segment of the population (the creditworthy/people with bank accounts/teenagers/families with children)?
- Customers who use a particular distribution channel (retail branches/ people with Internet access)?

All of these definitions of the market will be valid for particular purposes: some banks, for example, will only offer lending products to existing customers with a proven credit history. Normally, the reason for this policy is a conservative attitude to risk.

Note, however, that this approach will limit the potential market, and there can be a real danger of losing potentially profitable business to other less risk-averse institutions: in the corporate payment card arena, for example, many European banks have been cautious about entering a valuable market which American Express has consequently dominated. The point is that attitudes to risk and reward will vary, and will consequently have a very direct effect on market definition.

Occasionally, an institution will from the outset define the market for a particular product as crossing national boundaries: UK examples would include the 'offshore' savings products offered in the Channel Islands, and Euro-denominated bank accounts. Establishing market size for these transnational products poses particular challenges. For instance, a potentially valuable segment for them will be expatriates. But what does expatriates mean? Those who permanently live abroad? Or those who have been temporarily assigned overseas by their company? Would retired or working expatriates offer better prospects? Will sales be limited to UK nationals? How would we communicate and distribute the product to them?

'How big is the market?' also implies yet another question: 'What do we mean by big?' Size, of course, can be defined in a number of ways, but common measures are:

- financial volume, or total sales

- number of units sold

- number of customers.

In the case of financial services, all three provide useful and complementary insights:

Financial volume or total sales is helpful in determining the overall scale of the business, together with its potential for generating profit. Accordingly, when considering whether it should enter the fleet management services business, a company in the vehicle leasing industry wanted to know how much fleet operators spent on fuel, insurance and maintenance, because these three expense categories would make up the vast majority of the new service's billing revenue.

Number of units sold provides a guideline for assessing the operational impact on customer service departments. For example, a property and contents insurance application will have been reviewed, underwritten if necessary, quoted, passed through account set-up and policy issue, before the regular account maintenance tasks of registering name and address changes, alterations to direct debit mandates, and renewals. Managers in operations will need to know expected business volumes so that they can plan resource allocations.

Number of customers again provides a measure of scale, but also gives an indication of the product's potential to help the broader organisation grow by generating new customers who can be cross-sold other services. For instance, Centrica, originally a utility company which de-merged from British Gas, eventually included the AA (motoring services), One.Tel (telecoms) and CentricaGoldfish (credit cards and banking) in its product range with the specific goal of cross-selling them to its customers.

The Scope for Cross-selling

Cross-selling – the attempt to have an existing customer buy more than one product from you – has been a Holy Grail for the financial services industry since the first Florentine banker offered to make payments to a depositor's order.

Unfortunately, performance has often lagged behind aspiration: while 50 per cent of Abbey National customers have bought more than one product from them (*The Economist,* 1 March, 2003), the corresponding figure at Tesco Financial Services is only 12 per cent (*Financial Times*, 30 October 2002). Since its launch, Sainsbury's Bank has signed up 1.4 million customers but it still has a long way to go to hit its target of selling to between 20 and 25 per cent of the 10 million customers that visit its supermarkets each week (*Marketing Week*, 30 January 2003). Similarly, a scant 265 000 of Marks and Spencer's 6 million banking customers have taken out M&S personal loans (*The Economist*, 23 November 2002).

Compare this with the performance of Banco Popular, Spain's most efficient bank, which estimates that it places an average of seven financial products with each business client – more than double that of competitors (*Financial Times*, 16 August 2002).

Part of the reluctance of customers to flock to the one stop financial supermarket concept is a very understandable concern about having too many monetary eggs in one basket. Equally, it also has to be said that in-house products and services have too often been second rate. Consequently, the move to what is sometimes called 'open architecture', where the best product available on the market is offered under the provider's own label, should help cross-selling efforts. The Barclays Managed Account Program, for example, allows its affluent customers to place their investments in the hands of one of a range of independent asset managers from around the world.

The dimension which should not be forgotten in all this is time: we need to know, not only whether the market is big enough today to be interesting, but whether it has shown (or is likely to show) a consistent pattern of growth, so that it is likely to continue to be attractive over at least the medium term. Accordingly, market sizing estimates should go back perhaps five years and be supported by whatever evidence is available to forecast future growth. The forms such evidence might take are shown in Figure 4.1.

WHO ARE OUR COMPETITORS?

After building estimates of market size and dynamics, the next questions are 'Who are the key players? What is their market share?'

Just as it is important to ensure that the market definition we are using reflects reality, it is crucial not to define too narrowly who are our competitors. Attracted by the strong growth of the financial services industry, businesses in other, more mature

Evidence of growth	Example
The number of customers who meet this profile is growing	An increasing number of retired people boosts demand for home equity withdrawal products
This product meets an emerging need	Rising veterinary bills fuel the need for pet health insurance
This product is being bought because it is more effective and/or attractive than an earlier version	Mortgages with fixed interest rates offer more certainty than variable rate products
The market is changing in a way which will increase sales of this product	Less generous company pension provision increases demand for personal schemes
Emerging technology makes this product possible	The Internet enables online banking
A major competitor is likely to exit the market	RBS/NatWest quits investment banking

Figure 4.1 Market growth indicators

sectors have been tempted to join in the fray. In the UK, for example, the two leading supermarket chains have launched financial services products, as have M&S and Boots. Great things were hoped for from these developments: in 1998, Merrill Lynch forecast that by 2003, Tesco Financial Services would be generating a profit of £170 million, while its close rival J Sainsbury would be not far behind at £135 million. In the event, the pace of change was rather slower: Tesco's 2001 profits from the division came in at £40 million, while the corresponding figure at Sainsbury was £22 million; for its part, Boots terminated its credit card joint venture with Egg. But banks should not draw too much comfort from these results: the fact remains that Tesco, previously simply a supermarket, has sold financial products to 2.57 million of its 12 million customers, including more than 1 million credit cards, 500 000 car insurance policies, 200 000 general insurance products and even 50 000 life insurances ('Banking on Supermarkets' *Financial Times*, 30 October 2002).

Finding answers to the question 'What is the key players' market share?' can be as easy as buying an existing research study. In some segments, however, no material is available, and it becomes necessary to build one's own estimates of the overall market size and what portion of it may be held by competitors. This process is covered in the later section on quantitative research.

Having identified the current (and future) market leaders, it can be valuable to ask, 'What is their business strategy?' Firstly, of course, we can learn from the experience of those who are already operating in the market. However, understanding competitors' business strategy may also help by highlighting what they are not doing: we can therefore possibly identify an approach which no one is yet using. For instance, many sectors of the insurance market exploit the opportunity to sell their products through groups – charities, company employees, professional associations, car enthusiasts' clubs, trades unions and so on – by offering them a discount and/or a contribution to the organisation. Particularly successful with motor, household and travel insurance products, this 'affinity group' approach has also driven the growth of MBNA, a leading payment card issuer. Perhaps this is a strategy with potential for our particular market which has not yet been deployed: recent research suggests that 80 per cent of affinity groups have no relationship with financial services providers (*Wise Marketer*, 30 October 2003, quoting *Datamonitor: Affinity Marketing in UK Financial Services 2003*). An assessment of competitors' business strategies will help spot unexploited opportunities or distribution channels.

A competitive review will certainly also include an analysis of competitors' products; this should focus on price, target market, features and benefits, and distribution channels. It would also be valuable to consider their strengths and weaknesses, and perhaps even rank them in terms of the threat they offer to our own product. Figure 4.2 shows a possible approach.

At best, an analysis of this sort, valuable though it is, can only provide a snapshot of where the market is today. The financial services industry is so vulnerable to change – imposed by demographics, technology, shifts in legislation, emergence of new channels, mergers, sudden exposure to foreign competitors – that an assessment of these factors is crucial in trying to predict the long term strength of the new business.

CHANGES LIKELY TO AFFECT THE NATURE OF THE BUSINESS

DEMOGRAPHICS

In many European markets, the population is growing older. Largely driven by improvements in medicine, together with a trend for smaller families, started later, this change is already having significant effects on the financial services industry. For example, life insurers find that their customers are living – and drawing their pensions – for longer, while health insurers report that claims are increasing in both number and cost.

Similarly with changes in employment patterns: partly as a result of the increasing number of women who enjoy high salaries, there are now more wealthy women in the UK than men. A recent survey indicates that almost 300 000 women own at least £200 000 in cash, shares and bonds compared with just 271 000 men (*Wise Marketer*, 15 September 2003, quoting *UK High Net Worth Customers 2003*, Datamonitor).

Simply to remain in business, it is crucial to watch these changes carefully, and take whatever steps are necessary to reflect them. A more pro-active policy – positively searching out demographic and social changes, and developing products that match

Lender	Volume[1]/ Share %	Product name	Price	Features	Channel	Strategy	Strengths	Weaknesses	Threat ranking
A	£500m/37%	Golden Tracker	Base +0.8%	Fixed for life of mortgage; No costs	All	High value; heavy promotion	Strong presence in all distribution channels	High distribution costs	1
B	£350m/26%	Acme	Base +0.7%	Fixed for 3 years; Free valuation and legal	Internet only	Focus on younger buyers; aim to cross-sell	Heavily promoted to young affluent buyers	Footloose, price-sensitive customers	2
C	£100m/7%	Bestbuy	Base +0.5%	Fixed for 12 months	Branches only	Remain competitive	Regional player	Not a national player	3
Others[2]	£400m/30%								
Total	**£1.35bn**								

Source: Wondadata Quarterly Panel. Last updated 1 April 2004

[1] Annualised new loan volume.
[2] 17 in total, largest has 5% share.

Figure 4.2 Competitor analysis: tracker mortgages

them – has been the foundation of many new businesses: pet insurance is a profitable case in point.

TECHNOLOGY

The impact of the ATM on branch banking is well understood: without this alternative means of providing customer service, retail banks would never have been able to reduce so sharply their dependence on costly High Street bricks and mortar.

Following the success of ATMs, and then telephone banking, their next venture in remote servicing, banks have also had high hopes of dealing with as many as possible of their customers through the Internet. Clearly influenced by the calculation that it is 60 per cent cheaper for a branchless bank to gain a new customer than it is for a High Street bank (*Marketing Week*, 30 January 2003), some have taken the route of setting up an entirely new, separately branded business (for example, in Spain, SCH's Patagon and BBVA's Uno-e, and in the UK, Abbey National's cahoot). Others, more cautious, have simply added an online servicing capability to their existing channels (for example, Barclays, BNP Paribas). In both cases, once the high set-up expense has been absorbed, the ability to offer web-enabled account application, decisioning, set-up, transaction processing and routine maintenance has very sharply reduced back office costs for all kinds of financial services offerings. What is less clear is whether this is a new business, as sometimes claimed, or an old one with a new distribution and servicing method – and a profit-sapping need for very heavy marketing budgets. Evidence is also emerging that Internet applicants for lending products tend to have weaker credit histories and are more price-sensitive than conventionally recruited customers. As a result, the expectation in some quarters that branch banking would wither on the vine has clearly not been met. Instead, what we see is a combination of the two – 'clicks and mortar', as it is known.

Similarly, the 'pure play' Internet banks appear to be finding a limit to their ability to expand, once the first rush of early adopters has been recruited.

Again, WAP (Wireless Application Protocol) has failed to fulfill early predictions that it would revolutionise electronic banking: in the UK, both Abbey National and Halifax shut down their WAP banking services at the end of June 2003. (Abbey also closed its digital TV banking service.) This left just three WAP services running – from Nationwide, First Direct and cahoot – and cahoot was warning that its programme was under threat from lack of consumer take up (*New Media Age*, 16 June 2003).

All this may mean, however, is that the hot air has been squeezed out of the system: it does not change the long-term cost advantage to be gained from having customers do their own account servicing electronically.

When properly understood as a distribution medium rather than a new product, it is imperative that the effect of electronic channels is taken into account during the market planning process.

SHIFTS IN LEGISLATION

Few industries are as exposed to sudden changes in their legislative environment as financial services. Nor is this vulnerability likely to change soon. The pension funding problems overshadowing many European markets, the insurance mis-selling scandals in the UK, the emergence of strong and pro-active regulatory authorities are among the many influences which make it very important for the business plan to allow for the possibility that new legislation may fundamentally change the nature of the market. Not that this should always be understood as a threat: in fact, changes in the law can be among the most valuable business opportunities for companies which can move quickly to exploit them.

EMERGENCE OF NEW CHANNELS

Although distribution is closely connected with the question of technology, not all new channels are mediated by the electron. Banks and building societies (savings and loans in the US) are increasingly using their branch estate as a vehicle through which to sell products and services which at one time would have been thought to be too specialist for such treatment: one example is stock-broking services. Consequently, in early 2004 US banks were predicted to spend as much as $1.4 billion over the next two years in re-equipping some 30 000 branches to take on this new added-value sales and service centre role (*Qualisteam* 28 January 2004, quoting Datamonitor). Similarly, lending products have been sold directly in such non-traditional locations as railway stations and airports by specially trained third party sales forces.

Potentially even more important is the entry of big retailers into the financial services industry. According to Mintel, the equivalent of 9.3 million UK adults – one-fifth of the adult population – have purchased at least one financial product from non-traditional financial services institutions. But retailers still only represent 2–3 per cent of the overall banking sector (*Marketing Week*, 30 January 2003). Apart from the Sainsbury and Tesco forays already mentioned, supermarkets Safeway and Morrisons have also moved into the market through partnerships with Abbey National and HSBC respectively. At the time of writing, Asda only offers travel and pet insurance, but is rumoured to be recruiting senior retail financial services experts. Asda's US parent company, Wal-Mart, already offers own-branded ATMs, money orders and payroll cheque cashing.

Responding to these emerging pressures, in many markets banks have moved aggressively into residential mortgages, an area they were previously content to leave to building societies and savings banks. Buoyed by early success, some of them have begun to offer unsecured personal loans to the mass market, a business traditionally thought to be too risky for all but specialist lenders.

In fact, the emergence of new distribution channels can be as much a matter of creative thinking as of huge investments in new technology. For instance, telephone companies have enormous experience in charging and collecting payment for very low value transactions: there is real potential here for them to offer their billing capabilities in a business-to-business, business-to-consumer, or even consumer-to-consumer context. Once they gain momentum and credibility, it may be that they will begin to challenge the financial services industry's current monopoly on payment processing.

While it is understandable that some marketers will see the emergence of new channels as a threat, the more open-minded will realise that they offer an opportunity which may usefully be exploited to gain a competitive edge, or to defend an existing business. It makes sense to consider growth plans in the light of all the distribution channels which an organisation – or a competitor – could use.

MERGERS AND ACQUISITIONS

Financial service institutions merge with each other, partly of course to cut costs, but often with equal emphasis on adding customers and extending product range. This is what lay behind the once much-touted phenomenon of 'bancassurance', where banks have merged with or acquired insurance companies in order to sell their products to their banking customers. But the idea is of course capable of being applied in other areas: in the UK, for example, Barclays has bought the Woolwich Building Society specifically to be able to sell the latter's home loan products to its customers. Similarly, BNP Paribas has identified the European vehicle leasing and management industry as a prime investment target, and has acquired a number of companies to help it establish market dominance.

Sceptics will take grim satisfaction in the Boston Consulting Group's finding that, of 277 large mergers and acquisitions in the US between 1985 and 2000, 64 per cent destroyed value for the acquirers' shareholders (*The Economist*, 12 July 2003). But the point for marketers to note is that sensible, well-managed mergers and acquisitions can provide a fast way into a new business – or can re-energise hitherto somnolent or failing competitors.

As an example of a highly successful acquisition, consider HSBC's 2003 acquisition of Household Finance for $14 billion: undertaken to increase the bank's presence in the US, it also handily cut Household's annual funding costs by $1 billion (HSBC being a better risk than Household), and its administrative expenses by $200 million from integrating computer systems and cutting central costs. Further, HSBC expects to use the Household brand as a springboard into mass market consumer finance around the world (*Reuters*, 4 August 2003). The power of this ability to reach markets which HSBC itself cannot easily access is neatly illustrated by a pilot which the group carried out in Cambridge: would-be borrowers who were declined by HSBC were automatically referred to Household; out of every 20 applications so far, Household has approved 11 (*Financial Times*, 19 September 2003).

SUDDEN EXPOSURE TO FOREIGN COMPETITORS

In many markets, government policy has been deliberately aimed at protecting domestic financial service institutions from overseas competition. The efforts of the EU to create a single market for financial services throughout Europe will eventually sweep away many barriers, though the process seems likely to take some time. Still, in many countries and sectors, foreign competition – ambitious, amply resourced, and highly experienced – has already changed forever the nature of the business. In the UK payment card industry, for example, the arrival of the US monolines (specialist card issuers) with their aggressive acquisition campaigns has fundamentally changed the competitive playing field for the existing, predominantly bank-led players.

Similarly, SCH, the Spanish bank, has a substantial operation in Germany and with its major domestic competitor BBVA is now a leading player in Argentina and Mexico. Conversely, in their home territory, both SCH and BBVA have to contend with new entrants such as Barclays and Abbey National. And very few markets of any size fail to have at least a token presence from Citigroup.

No longer is it possible to rely on a relative lack of competition in a given market: the arrival of new entrants, even if ultimately they are not all successful, will transform customer expectations of what is possible in pricing and service. These eventualities must be factored in when assessing future market dynamics.

BARRIERS TO ENTRY

On the other hand, it is not always easy to break into a new market: there may be a number of factors which favour the existing players.

OPERATING LICENCES

To enter many sectors in the financial service industry (banking, for example) requires a licence to be issued from government or quasi-statutory bodies. Even where there is no undue delay in the process, existing competitors may be alerted to the development, and can make their plans accordingly.

In some developing markets, the number of operating licences granted to foreign competitors is deliberately limited in order to allow local providers to emerge. These restrictions may also be supplemented by other rules designed to restrict the activities of non-domestic operators. In China, for example, foreign insurers anxious to meet the rapidly growing market for life insurance products are restricted by regulations which only sanction branch openings in one location at a time. There are further rules specifying the instruments in which premium income can be invested. Equally challenging is the requirement for foreign insurers to enter into a joint venture with a domestic organisation whose main business is not insurance (*The Economist*, 20 September 2003).

ACCESS TO INFRASTRUCTURE

Certain sectors of the industry rely very heavily on an extensive operating infrastructure, such as that built to support cheque settlement, or mutually owned credit bureaux and insurance claimant databases. Normally the result of long-term industry investment, and virtually impossible to replicate at affordable cost, access to this infrastructure is often in the hands of a trade body which can move at its own pace in granting membership to new entrants

BUILDING DISTRIBUTION CHANNELS

It is expensive to build a retail branch network; creating a skilled sales force takes time and money. Even Internet sites are relevant only to that section of the market which has Internet access. As the table in Figure 4.3 shows, computer ownership and Internet access are high in Denmark, but much lower in France.

	Absolute figures		
	2000	2001	2002
Mexico	–	6.2	–
Turkey	6.9	–	–
Czech Republic	–	–	16.4
Portugal	8.0	18.0	–
France	11.9	17.8	–
Germany	16.4	27.0	43.3
Italy	18.8	–	–
United Kingdom	19.0	40.0	49.7
Austria	19.0	–	30.8
Ireland	20.4	–	–
Finland	30.0	39.5	44.3
Australia	33.0	–	–
New Zealand	–	37.4	–
Japan	34.0	35.1	48.8
Switzerland	36.5	–	–
Canada	40.0	48.7	–
Netherlands	41.0	–	–
United States	41.5	50.5	–
Denmark	46.0	59.0	–
Sweden	48.2	53.3	–

Source: OECD, ICT database, June 2003.

Figure 4.3 Percentage of all households having access to the Internet

In the first quarter of 2004, 49 per cent of households in the UK (12.1 million) could access the Internet from home, compared with just 13 per cent (3.2 million) in the same quarter of 1999 (see Figure 4.4).

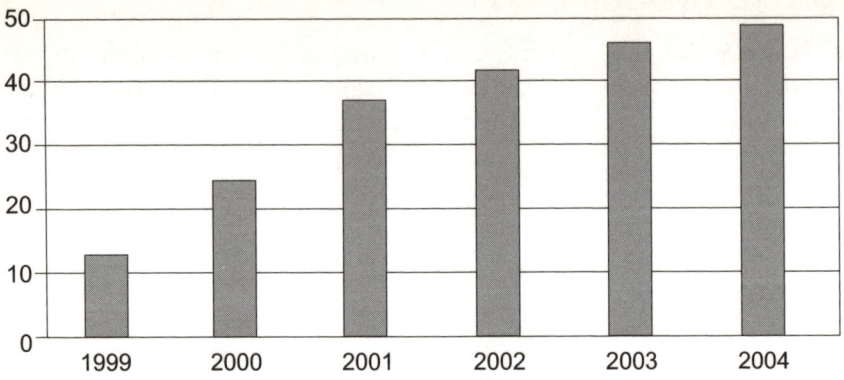

Source: Office for National Statistics, National Statistics Omnibus Survey

Figure 4.4 UK households with home access to the Internet, January to March

In April 2004, 56 per cent of adults in Great Britain had used the Internet in the three months prior to interview. The most common use of the Internet among this group was e-mail (85 per cent). Half (50 per cent) of all adults who had used the Internet in the three months prior to interview used it to buy or order tickets, goods and services.

Just over a quarter of adults in Great Britain (26 per cent) accessed the Internet every day or almost every day, while only 4 per cent accessed the Internet less than once a month.

Crucially, however, in April 2004, 39 per cent of adults had never used the Internet. Of these, 48 per cent stated that they did not want to use, or had no need for, or no interest, in the Internet; 38 per cent had no Internet connection; and 35 per cent felt they lacked knowledge or the confidence to use it. These adults were also asked which of four statements best described what they thought about using the Internet. Fifty-five per cent of non-users chose the statement 'I have not really considered using the Internet before and I am not likely to in the future'. *Source*: Office for National Statistics, Family Expenditure Survey/Expenditure and Food Survey.

While the Internet, direct mail and call centres offer attractive alternatives to building a branch network, they are not appropriate for all market segments: as a case in point, the wealthy will expect to receive a service demonstrably better than that offered to mainstream customers. In one Middle Eastern country, for example, the branches of a leading bank are provided with a specially furnished set of offices to receive their most affluent customers.

Drawing these threads together, it appears that the basic question of 'How big is the market?' in fact begs a whole array of questions to do with definitions and the present and future operating environment. To provide answers, financial services marketers usually need to do some research.

QUANTITATIVE RESEARCH

Establishing market size and growth prospects is one of the most important elements in quantitative research, and an essential first step in assessing business viability. Essentially, there are three main sources of information:

- data in the public domain and freely available
- published reports available for a fee
- specially commissioned research.

DATA IN THE PUBLIC DOMAIN AND FREELY AVAILABLE

In the UK, the most extensive source of data in the public domain is the government, which regularly produces surveys on a whole range of subjects relevant to the financial services industry. Usually, these reports can be very simply downloaded from the Internet; even more valuable, much of the data are available in spreadsheet format which makes it possible to do one's own calculations, produce charts and so on. Apart from the published research reports which are available either free or for a very modest fee, the Office for National Statistics (or other department producing the material) may be prepared to undertake some manipulation of the raw data to answer particular queries, again, either free or for a modest charge. My own experience of UK Government statisticians is that they are efficient, helpful and generally a pleasure to deal with. Other countries are not so well served.

Trade associations such as the British Bankers' Association and the Council of Mortgage Lenders also collect valuable data on their industries, as do commercial organisations which from time to time publish research on areas in which they have an interest. For example, Lex Vehicle Leasing produces a regular report on fleet management costs, which includes commentary on changing patterns of fleet finance. Commercially sponsored research of this sort can provide very useful insights, but may need to be approached with caution as its aim will usually be to promote the interests of the company sponsoring it.

General business publications and trade magazines are another valuable source of information: *The Banker*, the *Financial Times*, and *The Economist*, for instance, produce regular, authoritative reviews of issues relevant to the financial services industry.

Publicly available data are often no further away than an easily identified website. In some cases, however, it will not be obvious where the data are held. In that case, and especially if you need to make international comparisons, it may be necessary to work with a research organisation with special expertise in sourcing information.

PUBLISHED REPORTS AVAILABLE FOR A FEE

In the payment card industry, for example, estimates of issuer share are published annually by the Lafferty Group in its reports on key markets around the world. In other sectors, trade associations sometimes make available their own estimates of share. Since these reports have often been published for a number of years, it is also possible to build up a good idea of what is happening to the leading players' share over time. Industry-specific reports also often provide well-informed commentary on the strategies being followed by the most important competitors: this is invaluable in helping understand the business. Companies specialising in consumer information can usually provide useful estimates of market size and vendor performance. Commercially produced reports are rarely cheap, so, before buying, it is sensible to check the statistical basis on which they have been produced; if possible, ask to see a sample chapter. There is some surprisingly slipshod material on the market.

SPECIALLY COMMISSIONED RESEARCH

Inevitably there will be areas, often to do with product take-up or other measures of individual organisations' performance, which are not covered by either public domain data or industry reports. In that case, participating in an omnibus survey may be a cheap and quick solution.

An omnibus survey is usually repeated at regular intervals, and run by a market research company on behalf of a number of participants, who can nominate a fixed number of questions. Its main attractions are that it is much less expensive than dedicated research, the sample is usually quite large, and the regular repetition allows for valuable comparisons over time. On the other hand, it is not very flexible: the sample design is usually more or less fixed, and the number of questions is limited. Its main value is either in getting a quick fix on straightforward issues, or acting as a panel to provide ongoing measurements of attitudes, product take-up or brand share.

For more detailed investigations of either market size or market share, there is probably no substitute for specially commissioned research, despite its cost and the length of time it often will take to deliver results. Some research companies are generalists, others specialise in the financial services industry; which to select is largely a matter of personal preference and the type of survey involved, although choosing a specialist can save time at the initial briefing stage. In either case, you should plan to spend a great deal of time in explaining the business background to the project manager and his team. Only when you are completely confident that they know what you are trying to discover, and understand why, should you let them move to the issues of sample structure and questionnaire design.

Structuring the sample should present few problems, provided you bear constantly in mind who are the people you really want to talk to. Creating the questionnaire is less straightforward: not only is it essential to ask all the questions you want to ask (and no others – questionnaires have a bad habit of growing), it is also crucial to ask them clearly. In this connection, before clearing the questionnaire for the field it is no bad thing to test it on someone who has had nothing to do with developing it: this process can often show up unexpected ambiguities in the wording.

Multinationals can often be tempted to save time and money by working with a research company and/or questionnaire used in another market. Leaving aside the real issues posed if translation is necessary (a generalist translator may not have the expertise to deal with specialist topics), there can be important differences in market custom, products and nomenclature. For instance, North Americans and Germans mean rather different things when they speak of credit cards, and a New York research company which is entirely familiar with the mutual funds industry in the US may find itself having to start all over if it should have to replicate a US project in Europe.

SUMMING UP

In summary, in building our understanding of the potential viability of our product, we need to answer some basic questions:

- How big is the market? Is it likely to grow, remain static or shrink?

- Who are the main competitors? What is their strategy and how well are they doing?

- Is it possible to foresee any changes in the future which may have a significant effect on the business?

- Are there any barriers to entering this market?

In general, we can look to quantitative research to provide answers to many of these questions.

CHAPTER 5

Pricing the Product

INTRODUCTION

The importance of pricing strategy is sometimes underrated, but Figure 5.1 demonstrates the arithmetic fact that a small increase in price will have a larger effect than a similar cut in costs.

	Base case	Raise price by 1%	Cut costs by 1%
Selling price	100	101	100
Costs	80	80	79.2
Profit	20	21	20.8
Increase in profitability		5.0%	4.0%
Advantage of price increase		25.0%	

Figure 5.1 The importance of pricing strategy

Price setting is one of the most difficult decisions a marketer has to make: profitability depends on it, and prices, once set, can be difficult to change. Furthermore, while the accountant may propose a price, it is the customer who will decide whether or not to pay it. In practice, pricing decisions, while rooted in financial analysis, must be made in the light of judgements about the target market, about the competition, about product content, about positioning and about distribution.

Consequently, the discussion in this chapter inevitably will refer to topics which are dealt with more fully in other sections.

THE GOALS OF PRICE SETTING

Prices, then, must reflect both financial and marketing considerations.

FINANCIAL CONSIDERATIONS

These entail ensuring that costs are fully recovered, and that the margin will deliver an acceptable return given the product's risk profile, and the assets to be invested.

Chapter 6 on Assessing Business Performance makes a number of suggestions for financial measures.

One tool which is often used in price setting is break even analysis: break even comes when total sales revenue equals total cost, two terms which we need to define.

Total sales revenue may be expressed as price per unit multiplied by number of units. It will be sensible to explore a range of possible prices, together with estimates of what number of units could be sold at those prices.

Total cost is made up of fixed costs and variable costs:

- *Fixed costs* are the same at all sales levels. Examples of fixed costs would be an insurance company's sales force, a bank's branch network, and the occupancy costs of a call centre.

- *Variable costs* vary directly with sales. Examples would include commissions paid to intermediaries, cost of funds and 'welcome packs'.

In deciding where to allocate a particular cost, the time period involved has a role to play: over a ten-year period, even the size of a branch network can change dramatically, while a sales force can be scaled up or down in a matter of months. The best solution is to choose the time period most appropriate to the project. This will also help to determine whether an advertising budget, for example, should be treated as a fixed or variable cost.

Figure 5.2 illustrates the concept by showing that, for a given set of fixed and variable costs, break even can come at different levels of units sold, depending on what price is set. Accordingly, at a price of £2.6, we will need to sell 500 units to cover all our costs; at £3.5, around 300 units; and at £5, only 200 units.

				Sales revenue		
Units sold	Fixed cost	Variable cost	Total cost	Price A 2.6	Price B 3.5	Price C 5.0
100	800	100	900	260	350	500
200	800	200	1000	520	700	1000
300	800	300	1100	780	1050	1500
400	800	400	1200	1040	1400	2000
500	800	500	1300	1300	1750	2500
600	800	600	1400	1560	2100	3000
700	800	700	1500	1820	2450	3500
800	800	800	1600	2080	2800	4000
900	800	900	1700	2340	3150	4500
1000	800	1000	1800	2600	3500	5000
1100	800	1100	1900	2860	3850	5500
1200	800	1200	2000	3120	4200	6000
1300	800	1300	2100	3380	4550	6500

Figure 5.2 Finding the break even point (£)

Using the £2.6 price, the chart in Figure 5.3 makes the further important point that, at anything less than this level of sales, losses (the area between the total revenue and total costs lines) increase as sales fall, while above it, profit grows steadily in line with volume.

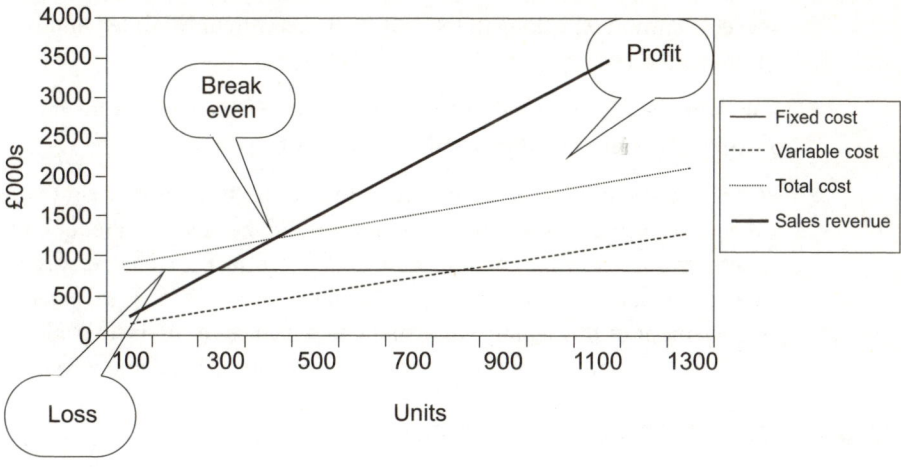

Figure 5.3   Finding the break even point

So far, the analysis has been financial. But it now becomes necessary to make a marketing judgement whether it is realistic to expect sales of 500 units at a price of £2.6. If not, the cost and revenue base will have to be revisited; if there is no possibility of reducing product expenses, then prices will have to be increased and/or more units will have to be sold – both moving the break even point. If none of these options is available, then the project will probably have to be abandoned. This is what happened in the case of Goldfish, a UK credit card brand, one of whose owners, Centrica, sold its 70 per cent share in the business to the 30 per cent partner, Lloyds TSB, because Goldfish had failed to reach its cash break even point (*Reuters*, 1 August 2003).

Note that higher risk products ought logically to carry a higher price. In fact, this is not often the case: a mainstream credit card will normally have the same APR for the majority of its cardholders. The 'risk-related pricing approach' is designed to charge better risk customers a lower rate of interest than those who have a patchy credit record. Reasonable as this risk/reward policy may be, it still incurs criticism from consumer advocates who argue, rather perversely, that it is confusing and discriminatory. Nevertheless, there is ample evidence to show that, properly managed, lending to 'sub-prime' customers, as they are known, can be quite profitable – without involving unacceptable risk levels or charging extortionate interest levels or fees. It also seems desirable that borrowers with impaired credit records should have the chance to take out loans, and rebuild their history. Equally, young people, who have had no opportunity to build up a financial history of any sort, will still need banking facilities and access to their cash: appropriate means must be found to make this possible.

Marketers have developed an array of price-led approaches to these challenges, which are intended to meet the customer need while at the same time safeguarding the interests of the financial services institution:

- low cost current (checking in the US) accounts with only limited and fully authorised access to cash

- sub-prime loans and credit cards, with higher APRs and fees for late or missed payments, overlimits and lower lines of credit

- secured loans and credit cards, where the account-holder is required to provide a cash deposit often to the value of the loan or credit limit. (Seemingly illogical for the consumer, this is in fact a valuable way for people with a poor credit record to rehabilitate themselves, as satisfactory management of this facility will usually be taken as prima facie evidence that the customer may now be offered a more conventional loan product.)

MARKET-ORIENTED CONSIDERATIONS

Once the financial context is understood, marketing considerations come into play. In most cases, this will mean taking proper account of what competitors are charging; but how this is achieved will often depend on the product's positioning. For example, a health insurance product targeted at young marrieds, whose main appeal is intended to be its affordability, will have to be pitched at or below the price charged by the market leader in that segment. On the other hand, a premium product, aimed at say the mass-affluent market, may even be set at a higher price than the competition, if the underlying customer proposition is felt to support this. An instance would be the American Express card, which in the UK charges a substantial annual fee for a product which gives access to only a small fraction of the merchants covered by the Visa or MasterCard networks, whose members' cards are usually issued free of an annual fee. Nevertheless, American Express is very successful in selling the card on the basis of the intangibles that customers feel it offers.

Assuming – as we must hope will be the case – that our product cost is less than the price our main competitors are charging for a similar product, a spectrum of pricing strategies is available, as represented in Figure 5.4.

Skimming

Setting the highest possible price in order to maximise profitability.

Premium

Charging more than the current generic market price, using superior quality (real or perceived) as a support.

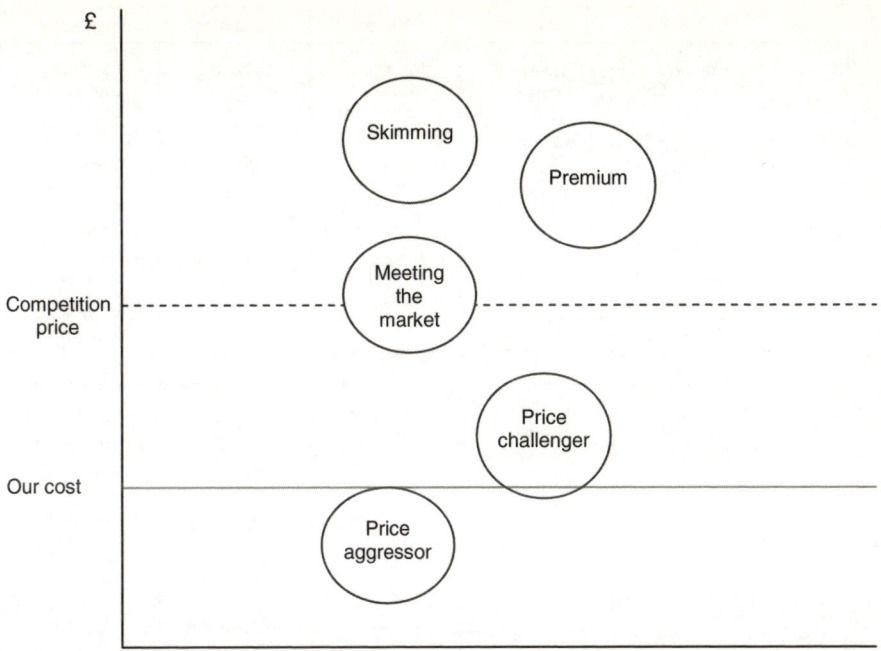

Figure 5.4 Spectrum of pricing strategies

Meeting the market

Pricing at much the same level as charged by the competition: a conventional route, which suggests that, if the product is to build share, it will have to be superior to its competitors in other ways – for instance, what it offers, how it is delivered or how it is promoted. On the other hand, it is not unknown for financial services institutions to create products which are there simply to meet, rather than beat the competition; in this case, market pricing would be the sensible option.

Price challenger

This option would normally imply that the product proposition is on a par with (or a little below) the typical market offering, and that either our product costs today are much lower than the competition, or are expected to be in the future as a result of economies of scale generated by creating new customers and acquiring them from competitors.

Price aggressor

The implication here is that, for a time at least, we are prepared to offer the product at a price below cost in order to gain share from existing incumbents. This option requires confidence in being a low cost producer – ideally, *the* low cost producer.

	Skimming	Premium	Market	Challenger	Aggressor
When	• No competition (first to market, legal protection, technical advantage) • Inelastic demand • Limited availability	• Superior product • Exceptional content • Upscale positioning	• Need to match competitive offerings • No compulsion to build share quickly • Product content at parity • To round out product range	• To build share • Value proposition at parity or lower • To create consumer recognition	• To dominate market • Strategy is to build profitability through high volume, low margin sales • Product at parity or lower • Entrenched competition
Pro	• Highly profitable	• Generates increased revenues at limited incremental cost	• Easy to sell, internally and externally	• Quickly builds visibility and volume • Popular with salespeople • Can be positioned as introductory offer	• High visibility • Fast results • May be only way for newcomer to break into tightly held market
Con	• May be unsustainable in the longer term as competitors erode advantage • May lead to negative PR	• Content and service must continuously justify premium price	• Unlikely to build commanding market position • May mask ignorance of market demand and of internal costs	• May attract price-conscious (and therefore footloose) rather than profitable customers	• Appeal may be more to price-conscious (and therefore footloose) rather than profitable customers • Needs unremitting attention to costs • May fail to generate sufficient volume
Example	• Stock issue underwriting fees • Money laundering	• Barclays Premier Banking, targeted at mass-affluent customers	• 'Me too' products of all kinds	• Egg savings products offered significantly better than market rates at launch	• US monolines breaking into previously bank-dominated UK card market

Figure 5.5 Pricing strategies compared

Note that it is often difficult, and in practice very unwise, to separate price from product content or product positioning. Even over a short period of time, charging a premium price for a non-premium product will not be supportable – at least, for businesses which value their reputation, or plan to have a future. Equally, it is prudent to be sure that a low price strategy is supported by low production and delivery costs.

LOW PRICE STRATEGIES

Carefully managed, low price strategies can be highly successful in the financial services industry.

This was the approach very successfully adopted by the US payment card specialists (the so-called 'monolines') when they entered the UK market: by offering the previously unheard of zero APR on balance transfers, together with temporary or permanent account fee waivers, aggressive newcomers such as Capital One were able to grab share away from complacent bank card issuers.

A very similar situation arose in the UK mortgage market (Figure 5.6). Starting in the early 1980s, High Street banks decided that they would begin to compete with building societies (savings and loans in the US) in the home loan market. Overwhelmingly, this competition took the form of lower APRs, fixed rates and/or cash inducements.

The result was that by 2001, all the top mortgage lenders bar one were either banks or the result of mergers between a bank and a building society (see Figure 5.7).

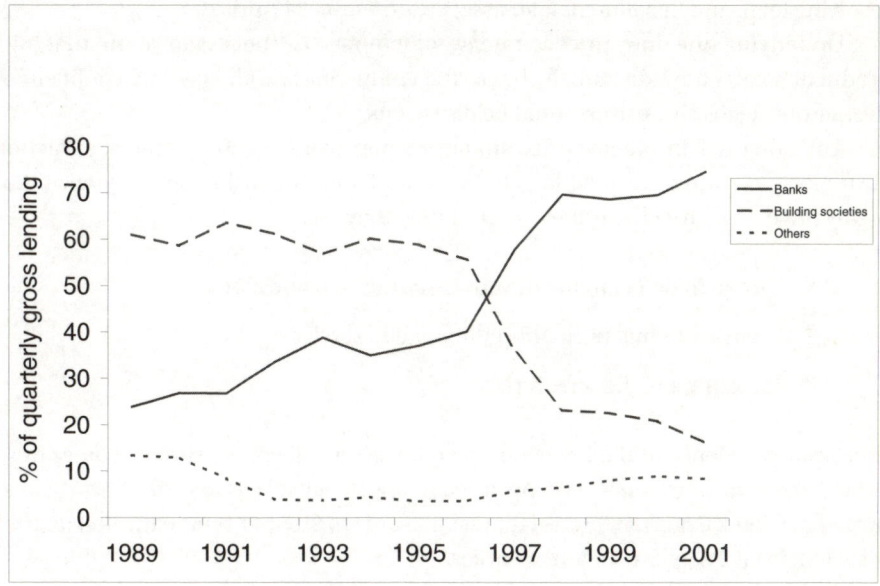

Source: Bank of England, *Annual Abstract of Statistics*

Figure 5.6 Percentage share of mortgage market by lender type

Total mortgage balances outstanding			
Rank	Name of group	£ billion	Estimated market share (%)
1	HBOS	129.3	21.9
2	Abbey National	73.3	12.4
3	Lloyds TSB	56.6	9.6
4	Barclays	51.0	8.6
5	Nationwide BS	49.1	8.3
6	The Royal Bank of Scotland	37.0	6.3
7	Northern Rock	22.6	3.8
8	Alliance & Leicester	22.0	3.7
9	HSBC Bank	16.7	2.8
10	Bradford & Bingley	16.1	2.7

Source: Council of Mortgage Lenders

Figure 5.7   Largest mortgage lenders 2001

Note that, even in experienced and capable hands, a low price strategy can take time to deliver profitability: from launch in 1998, Capital One's UK operation only moved into the black in 2002 – but in that time, and in a fiercely competitive market, they had captured 2.8 million accounts and £2.4 billion ($3.9 billion) in credit card, revolving loan, and installment loan assets (*CardFlash*, 24 April 2003).

Underlying the low price strategy, of course, is the assumption that our production costs are substantially below the competition. Unless we are confident of this, setting aggressive prices would be disastrous.

The other risk in the low price strategy is negative selection – that is, attracting customers who are motivated largely by price. There is considerable evidence that highly price-sensitive clients are less desirable; they are:

- prone to defect to the next price-cutter to come along;

- unlikely to buy profitable added-value services;

- possibly a higher credit risk.

Compelling evidence of the impact on margins of so-called 'rate surfers' comes from the US: the *Wall Street Journal* (25 April 2003) reported that 'These surfers have helped push down Bank One's net interest margin on cards to 8.16 per cent in the first quarter (of 2003), from 9.51 per cent a year earlier.'

For maximum market responsiveness, rate surfers must incur low or no switching costs (in fact, cash back offers can generate switching income), are fully aware of all the competitive offerings and are willing to take advantage of them.

This is not always the case. In the UK, both Cheltenham & Gloucester and Egg have successfully demonstrated that it is possible to attract savers by offering higher than market returns (the equivalent of lower price), and then over time reducing rates to 'normal' levels, trusting to inertia to retain a high proportion of the original accounts. In this case presumably, even aware investors have decided that switching to a more rewarding provider is not worth the effort.

For example, research by the consumer magazine *Which?*, suggested that a mere 3.5 per cent of current account customers at the big four UK banks might transfer to more competitive rivals. And even that very low rate is nearly three times that in a Department of Trade and Industry survey into switching behaviour in 2000: at that time, only 6 per cent of current account customers had transferred their accounts in the previous five years (*Financial Times*, 30 July 2002). This is a telling example of the 'stickiness' of savers and investors, once acquired.

And what is true of savers is also true of many borrowers: despite the lower APRs available elsewhere, mortgage broker Charcol found that 75 per cent of UK mortgage-holders never remortgage, and only 4 per cent have remortgaged more than once. As a result, based on the average UK home-loan, Charcol calculates that home-owners have failed to take advantage of £8.4 billion of savings (*Brighton Evening Argus*, 28 February 2003). This accords fully with the finding of a KPMG study that 54 per cent of respondents said that remortgaging was 'too much hassle for too little gain' (*Wise Marketer*, 25 February 2003.) Similarly, Egg has found that 87 per cent of credit card customers stay with the bank after the introductory rates expire (*Wall Street Journal*, 25 February 2002).

Taken together, the evidence seems to suggest that low price strategies will certainly attract rate surfers some of whom, having been expensively recruited, are likely to move to the next loss leader which comes along. However, the proportion may vary from product to product: Egg's experience was that only 13 per cent of credit card accounts moved on, and the Charcol survey found only 4 per cent of serial mortgagers among its respondents. On balance, therefore, provided the cost structure will support it, aggressive pricing followed by a gradual move to market pricing could well be an appropriate strategy for profitable market entry.

HIGH PRICE STRATEGIES

It is probably fair to say that most marketers are more familiar with building profitability through low prices and high volume than high prices and low volume. Yet, in the right context, a high price strategy can be the preferred option to maximise profit.

This is particularly the case where the product or service has a real or perceived advantage over the competition, and still more so where the supplier is in a quasi-monopolistic situation. In the financial services industry, competition and regulation ensure that there are very few examples of monopoly suppliers, although money launderers would probably qualify at least as oligopolists. Consequently, price skimming in its purest form is very seldom heard of. However, there are many examples of premium pricing, ranging from the private wealth management services offered in Switzerland and Liechtenstein, through the upgraded facilities offered by banks to their 'mass-affluent' customers, through to high-end property and contents insurance.

By offering enhanced services, all these offerings have the objective of attracting and retaining better-off customers and, by charging an appropriate fee for these services, providing them profitably.

There is an assumption here, however: that better-off customers are necessarily more profitable customers. Figures quoted for the Visa Infinite Card ('the most sophisticated credit card in the world...most exclusive services available... a select group of upscale consumers...unparalleled services and benefits...') when it was launched in France in 2003 seem to confirm that at the least, these are busy users (see Figure 5.8).

Card type	Annual transactions	Average transaction value	Annual billings
Visa Infinite	214	€100	€21 350
American Express	nk	nk	$7645
Co-brand/affinity	nk	$80.84	$5262
		(CardFlash 24 Aug 2000)	
Sub-prime	nk	nk	$1886

Source: Qualisteam 14 Mar 2003; American Express Annual Report 2002; CardFlash 13 Mar 2003

Figure 5.8 Card volumes compared 2002

But there is significant evidence from American Express in the US that more affluent customers do in fact generate substantial incremental revenues.

In 2000, American Express Financial Advisers (AEFA) launched a Platinum Financial Services product combining a Platinum Card, concierge services, financial planning and advice, banking, investment, insurance and trust services, plus a relationship manager. It targeted customers with more than $500 000 in assets. In test, Platinum clients invested an average $250 000 of new funds, a success which led to a national roll-out during 2001 (*American Express Annual Report 2001*). In the following year, the company chairman was able to report that 'AEFA clients who enrolled in Platinum Financial Services invested significantly more of their assets with us, and Platinum portfolios for new clients averaged nearly $1 million' (*American Express Annual Report 2002*).

Similarly, AEFA's ONE Financial Account is 'an integrated financial management tool' that combines its clients' investing, banking, lending and card relationships into a single account. Since launch, it has generated $2.2 billion in new funds. Average assets for ONE clients are four times higher than for other AEFA clients (*American Express Annual Report 2002*).

Clearly, the better-off have more potential than those less affluent for buying financial products. But the key must be to realise that potential, and then turn it into profit.

For example, a study by Oliver, Wyman & Company shows that online account aggregation can increase profitability per customer by $148 for retail banks and $178 for brokerages, with corresponding improvements in account retention. The study found that aggregation can increase retention to 94 per cent, compared to an average retention rate of 88 per cent for all other online customers including those who pay bills online. The relevant point for our purposes here comes from the finding that some 57 per cent of aggregation users have an annual household income greater than $75 000 compared with only 33 per cent of online banking households. (*CardFlash*, 28 October 2002). In other words, these performance improvements are the direct result of marketing upscale products to upscale clients.

Having once set a premium price for a product, it is crucial never to challenge it: nothing is more likely to jeopardise upscale positioning (and therefore upscale profitability) than price promotions or mass marketing.

A fine example of this comes from the US payment card market, where, in a bid to build share, aggressive issuers used the previously upscale Gold Card as a way to distinguish their acquisition mailings from those of their competitors. The result has been two fold: first, a steady decline in the status of the Gold Card, through being the standard offering down to its current position, where it is a featured product in the sub-prime market. The other consequence has been the need to create a replacement upscale offering. At first, this was Platinum, launched in 1996, but this product too began to be degraded: some sub-prime issuers, such as Capital One, offered Platinum cards with credit lines as low as $300, and Platinum cards of one sort or another were eventually held by nearly 60 per cent of all US households (*CardFlash*, 31 July 2003). Accordingly, a new higher Titanium tier was introduced – and First USA/Bank One promptly issued a student version of it (*Wall Street Journal*, 9 April 2002). Bowing to the inevitable in July 2003, Visa announced that it was merging its Classic, Gold, and Platinum products into one product stream. It remains to be seen whether the Visa Infinite card announced in 1998 will go the same way, or whether MasterCard has been able to impose more discipline on its members.

This is not absolutely to rule out price promotions, which have their place as a means of building short-term sales. Very great care is called for, however: unless they are strictly occasional and strictly temporary, price promotions will:

• devalue the brand;

• attract price conscious customers who may well not be either loyal or profitable;

• make it difficult to return to 'full price'.

On balance, unless there are very compelling reasons to offer even short-term price reductions on a premium product, it is probably wiser not to.

COMMUNICATING PRICES

In any product market, it makes good long-term sense to explain prices prominently and unambiguously. In the financial services industry, this sound practice is, in theory at least, very often reinforced by legislation aimed at ensuring complete clarity for the consumer. As these statutory requirements will vary from market to market – and often from time to time, as original formulations turn out to be faulty, or new developments force a re-think – it is impossible to make any detailed recommendations, other than to urge strongly a check on the current position either with in-house lawyers or direct with the regulatory authority.

RELATIONSHIP PRICING

Pricing in the corporate, or business-to-business market, however, is often less regulated. This does not mean that the same principles of clarity ought not to apply: but it does mean that clarity may be more difficult to arrive at. A corporation may be a customer of the institution for a number of different services, all provided by different divisions. Consequently, it may well be looking for this wide relationship to be reflected in the charges it pays. But each of the divisions will have its own cost and revenue dynamics, and the customer's importance to each division may vary. Deciding a price under these circumstances will be difficult, and is more likely to be judged by subjective than objective means. In the end, the customer's overall value to the institution must be the acid test, together with the risk of losing them.

Clarity need not necessarily mean a published price list: but it ought to mean, at least for internal use, a consistently applied set of rules for establishing charges. It should also mean that one person – the individual with overall P&L responsibility for

---

Getting Pricing Wrong/Pricing in a Panic

The bigger the customer, the more buying leverage they have, and many clients will use this aggressively.

I recall one instance of a customer who had a good idea that losing their business would be very damaging, not just to meeting our 'stretch targets' for sales growth, but could even hit very hard our existing business figure. Accordingly, they negotiated very toughly, and with some face-saving concessions, we agreed to their demands.

In retrospect, this was a mistake. Their defection would only have caused short-term damage; by driving a coach and horses through our entire pricing policy, we jeopardised the whole business.

the business unit – reviews all pricing agreements, and that only they have authority to vary the application of those rules. It is usually a bad idea to let sales people set prices.

It is also possible for the downwards pricing pressure to be led by the supplier, rather than demanded by the customer: for instance, when banks offer credit to blue chip companies, they keep their rates low, in the hope that later they will be awarded more profitable contracts, such as underwriting securities. For example, when in 2003 M&S negotiated a syndicated bank loan of £1.25 billion ($2 billion), the facility was priced at a very favourable rate: the banks charged 10 basis points for undrawn margins, 20 basis points over Libor (London Inter-bank Offered Rate) for anything drawn, with an additional 5 basis points charged if more than 50 per cent of the line was drawn. The arrangement was described as 'a relationship loan, granted by banks in the hope of getting ancillary business such as merger and acquisition banking and bond underwriting in the future' (*Financial Times*, 15 August 2003). The risk here, of course, is that the customer accepts the low-priced sprat, but fails to deliver the mackerel.

More murky is the practice of brokers offering free research to big investment clients such as pension funds: it is not at all clear whether this in the long-term public interest. Even less defensibly, in the frenzy of the dot.com boom investment bankers offered privileged positions in 'hot IPO offerings' to special customers.

BUNDLED PRICING

In some ways, bundled pricing is akin to relationship pricing, except that it starts with the product, rather than the customer. A product with a bundled price is one which brings together a number of separate services and charges only one price for them. In this sense, the American Express Platinum Financial Services and ONE Account products mentioned on page 52 have bundled pricing.

Another example would be the 'wrap fee' programmes which bring together a number of investment services, including buying and selling securities, for one fee, rather than charging separate commissions for each transaction. Evidence of the relevance of the bundling approach is the fact that, by the end of 2001, US investors held around $50 billion of assets in wrap-fee accounts, with a further $70 billion held by non-US savers (*Wall Street Journal*, 25 April 2002). In the UK, a Mintel survey found that 6 million bank customers have fee-based accounts, generating annual revenues of £600 million (*Marketing Week*, 30 July 2003).

A particular risk with bundled pricing comes when changed circumstances – increased cost or unexpectedly high usage, for example – make it necessary to begin to charge for an element that previously was provided without separate charge. Levying a fee for what was 'free' can be controversial: witness the furore in both the US and the UK when banks decided they would have to start charging (or charging a much higher price) for ATM transactions.

Essentially, bundled pricing relies on generating sufficient extra volume to offset the lower margins. It makes sense to check regularly that this is actually what is happening. One safeguard is to set minimum volume requirements; if these are not met, pricing then defaults to the unbundled level. For instance, in April 2002, the *Wall Street Journal* reported that the average minimum balance required by Internet banks to avoid fees on interest-paying accounts was $1239.10, up 49 per cent from the previous year.

UNBUNDLED PRICING

In a market which is dominated by bundled pricing, a new entrant can often win business by unbundling product charges. The argument here is that, rather than pay for services which the customer does not need, the customer should be able to choose only those which are relevant to them. Perhaps the best-known example comes from outside the financial services industry: historically, scheduled airline fares have included a wide array of services in addition to the cost of personal transportation. A 'full fare' air ticket from London to Paris will provide food, drink, baggage handling, some taxes, free transferability to other flights and even carriers, and full refund if it is not used. To offer a cheaper fare, low cost airlines usually exclude some or all of these extra benefits.

Some financial service institutions are moving closer to this position: for example, many banks now charge for services such as cheques or ATM transactions which would at one time have been seen as an integral part of providing current account services. But note that there is an important distinction between unbundling and simply introducing new charges.

Often enough, pricing in an industry can move back and forth between bundled and unbundled approaches, as new entrants focus successively on the convenience and simplicity of all-inclusive prices, and then on the transparency and flexibility of what is often called 'cafeteria pricing'. Take, for instance, a commentary from the *Financial Times* on approaches to charging securities buyers for investment research:

> As practices change, so will the industry's pricing model. Investment research has traditionally been bundled with equities sales and trading as a single service. A variety of new pricing models is bound to develop. In some cases, research will be charged for separately. In other cases, there will be tiered pricing for research, based on the amount of research and other services that an investor wants. Three tiers are likely to evolve: 'research light' for smaller clients; 'bespoke research' for larger clients; and the full tailored offer.
> (*Financial Times*, 30 April, 2003)

MIXED PRICE STRATEGIES

A mixed price strategy recognises that, properly priced, nearly all the segments of a market can be profitable – although to different extents. In fact, the argument has been made that the customers with the most profit potential are the less well off and the most affluent, leading to an hourglass effect, shown in Figure 5.9.

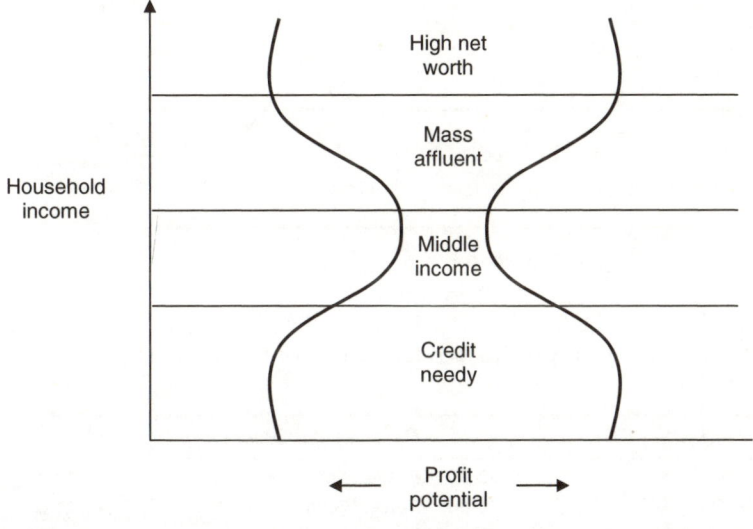

Figure 5.9 Profit potential by household income

The approach here is to develop a range of appropriately priced and designed products to meet the needs of each of these segments. The payment card industry has probably gone further than most to implement this strategy by creating a carefully planned hierarchy of products, shown in Figure 5.10. Each of these products will be marketed at a price point, and with a customer value proposition, which reflects the needs of the segment to which it is addressed.

For instance, in December 2001, the average rates of interest charged by different categories of credit card in the US are shown in Figure 5.11.

There are some notable features here:

1. Price should reflect risk: in other words, the more creditworthy the account, the lower the APR that needs to be charged. Generally, then, we should expect to see APRs falling as we move up the product hierarchy from Standard through Gold to Platinum. In fact, Platinum APR is higher than Standard, but Gold is higher than either. One reason is that Gold has been used as an acquisition device in the sub-prime market, which carries a higher APR.

2. In terms of the targeted customer type, student cards appear to be rated as

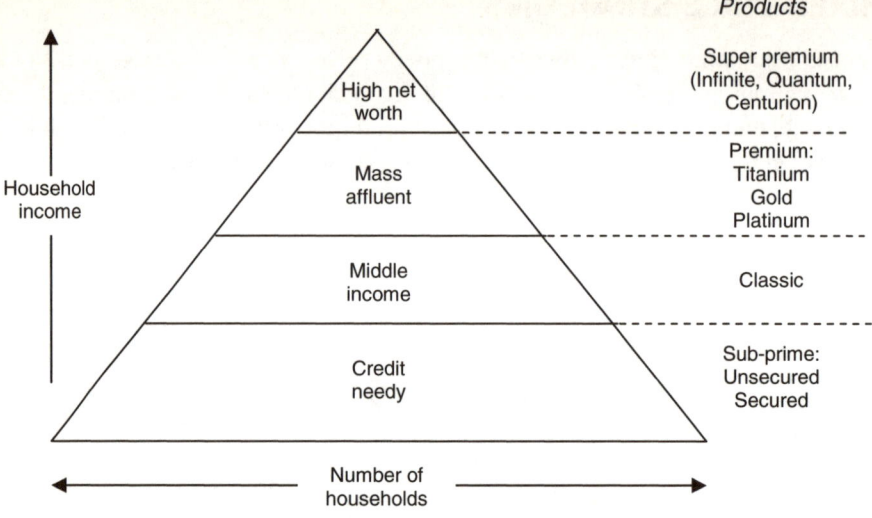

Figure 5.10   Theoretical hierarchy of products for the payment card industry

Cards by card type (%)		Cards by customer type (%)	
Overall Standard Card	15.95	Business Card	12.08
Overall Gold Card	16.66	Reward Card	14.65
Overall Platinum Card	13.28	Co-Branded Card	14.92
Low-Rate Standard	10.04	Student Card	15.43
Low-Rate Gold	10.48	Unsecured Sub-Prime	20.73
Low-Rate Platinum	11.30	Secured Sub-Prime	17.00

Source: CardFlash, 15 February 2002

Figure 5.11   Average rates of interest: US credit cards, December 2001

a higher credit risk than, say, business cards, but not as high as unsecured sub-prime cards, or still less secured sub-prime cards. This approach would seem intuitively to be sensible, especially given the priority which most financial services institutions place on student customers, many of whom, of course, will go on to be high earners and valuable customers.

3.   'Low rate' cards are marketed with a relatively low APR, but usually higher account fees and administrative charges; this reflects the increasing tendency to break away from fixed product content and to allow more customer choice.

Setting Prices for Multinational Buyers

Challenges to pricing policy can arise when important corporate customers operate in more than one country. In those circumstances, they will almost always seek to establish that the lowest price in any of the markets should be the price for all of them.

For example, if a multinational does business with a bank in countries around the world, it frequently happens that the fees charged in each of those markets vary very widely. This is likely to be a result of different operating costs, different levels of business (and therefore different volume discounts), different local price structures, and probably different levels of competition. Back at Head Office, the client corporation's purchasing managers will argue that local pricing should be abandoned: only one price should be set, and that the lowest. However, this may cause a major problem in individual markets, where the multinational can be dwarfed by big local customers who would certainly demand a still better deal if they got to hear of the arrangement, as they probably would. It may also be that local operating conditions make it impossible to support a bargain basement price.

One solution, which offers advantages to both parties, is to retain the local pricing structure, but to apply to it standardised discounts earned by the multinational's worldwide business volume.

CHOOSING A STRATEGY

Often enough, market conditions, together with the expense of producing, promoting and servicing the product will define the pricing strategy fairly conclusively. At other times, however, there may well be choices: this would be particularly true of a new or niche product for which the market has not yet established prices. In this case – and it would be appropriate even where the pricing strategy is clear – it will be necessary to do some modelling.

Some marketers are nervous about the whole notion of modelling. In fact, there is nothing mysterious about it, and spreadsheet programs make the process almost painless. Even examples as straightforward as those in Figure 5.12 demonstrate the power of this aid to business planning:

In Scenario A, the Market pricing strategy would be a clear winner. But Scenario B shows that even a relatively small change in the assumptions makes a large difference to the outcomes: a slightly more optimistic forecast about sales levels identifies Premium pricing as an alternative strategy worth exploring.

COMBINING THE FINANCIAL AND MARKETING APPROACHES TO PRICING

It would be wrong to set prices using only either financial or marketing criteria. For instance, the chart in Figure 5.13 is an overview of the main elements involved in pricing business cards (the business expense payment cards which many banks market to small companies).

Scenario A			
000 except price			
	Pricing strategy		
	Premium	*Market*	*Aggressive*
Price ($)	200	150	100
Sales (No. of units)	200	350	400
Total revenues ($)	*40 000*	*52 500*	*40 000*
Fixed costs ($)	30 000	30 000	30 000
Variable costs ($) ($60/unit)	12 000	21 000	24 000
Total costs ($)	*42 000*	*51 000*	*54 000*
Profit ($)	**-2000**	**1500**	**-14 000**

Scenario B			
000 except price			
	Pricing strategy		
	Premium	*Market*	*Aggressive*
Price ($)	200	150	100
Sales (No. of units)	220	350	400
Total revenues ($)	*44 000*	*52 500*	*40 000*
Fixed costs ($)	30 000	30 000	30 000
Variable costs ($) ($60/unit)	13 200	21 000	24 000
Total costs ($)	*43 200*	*51 000*	*54 000*
Profit ($)	**800**	**1500**	**-14 000**

Figure 5.12   Price strategy modelling

Customer	Product		Marketing	Factors affecting price				
Growth stage	Product type	Positioning		Relative credit risk	Funding costs	Financial		Income potential
						Account management and processing costs		
Mature	Credit card	For carefully-selected creditworthy companies	Acquisition cost: Channel used Channel efficiency Approval rate	Lower	Highest (driven by volume, days' grace and rollover behaviour)	Account management higher Volumes may be higher		High: Interest income Added value services Merchant charges
Transition	Charge card	For companies wishing more days' grace, with appropriate fee structure	Competition: Pricing Value proposition Client relationship	Medium	Medium (driven by volume and days' grace)	Account management higher Volumes may be higher		Medium: Added value services Merchant charges
Start up	Debit card	Entry level product for most small business customers		Higher	Lowest (direct debit to customer bank account)	Account management lower Volumes may be lower		Low: Merchant charges only – but note potential for selling lending products to qualified customers

Figure 5.13 Pricing business cards

SUMMING UP

It could be said that pricing is too important to leave to the accountants and too dangerous to be left to the marketers: it is imperative to set prices which recognise costs and maximise profitability, but the analysis must also reflect market realities. Profit can also be maximised in more than one way: there is a variety of strategies, each of which may be appropriate in different settings of demand and cost of supply. Modelling will help decide which option to follow.

Assessing Business Performance

INTRODUCTION

We live in a world which sets great store on transparency and accountability. An important consequence of this is that virtually any organisation has to be capable of reporting to the various groups which have a legitimate interest in it – 'stakeholders' in the current phrase – on its stewardship of the assets entrusted to it. This means that some agreement has to be reached on how to measure performance, and different types of organisation will often develop measures appropriate to their circumstances. For example, a library system may decide to compare the performance of its different sites by comparing how many books they lend out per head of the population which they serve. But this leads immediately to questions of definition: What do we mean by 'books'? Does this include video tapes? CDs? What do we mean by 'population served'? Apart from geographical difficulties of definition, there may well be significant differences in the type of population served: a performance which would be normal in a middle-class area may be out of reach in one which is educationally deprived. Famously, the introduction of performance measures in Britain's National Health Service has generated tremendous controversy.

Fortunately, the financial services industry has a whole toolbox of measures it can use – measures with generally agreed purposes and definitions – though even here, arguments about definition and suitability for a particular case are fairly common. Many of the yardsticks will be financial: the inputs are money, or can be measured in monetary terms, and financial measures have the advantage of flexibility: they can be used across many different kinds of business and even across national borders. Other criteria will assess how well the business is performing in the market place. Both types will be used by those who are concerned with understanding how well an established business or a new investment project is performing or will perform. And, since that business or that investment project will probably be only one of many in which the organisation can invest, for consistency it will want to use the same measures on all its actual or potential businesses or plans, so that it can be sure that it is generating the best value for its stakeholders. How businesses in the financial services industry do this is the subject of this chapter.

MEASURING SUCCESS

Success for a business can be defined in any number of ways: in one multinational financial services institution I am familiar with, reviews for a particular quite large business unit centred around the contribution it was making to the goals of the rest of the organisation. For a number of years, senior management expected no more of it than that it break even and help much more visible and profitable parts of the business make money.

This approach is unusual. More commonly, organisations in the financial services industry will use one or more of the following financial and marketing measures – or metrics as they are often called – to assess performance at both product and project level.

FINANCIAL MEASURES

EBITDA	Earnings before interest, taxes, depreciation and amortisation
EBIT	Earnings before interest and taxes
PTI	Pre-tax income
ROI	Return on investment
ROA	Return on assets
ROE	Return on equity
NPV	Net present value.

Each of these measures has its merits and its proponents, and this is not the place in which to enter into an essentially technical debate as to which is the most useful measure. Almost certainly, any financial service institution will have its own favoured in-house yardsticks and models. Generally, accounting measures commonly found in the financial services industry are PTI, ROA and NPV. These are valuable in the sense that they measure, respectively:

PTI	The absolute earnings of the business before the often arbitrary effect of taxation
ROA	The efficiency of the business at using the assets invested in it to make a profit
NPV	A business may be thought of as generating streams of profitability now and in the future. However, on the 'bird in the hand' principle, profit arising in the future is normally considered to be worth less than profit earned now. NPV is an umbrella term for a set of techniques whose purpose is to estimate what those future earnings may be worth today.

Additionally, for investment projects, 'pay-back period' is often calculated: this is the time it takes for expected profits generated by the project to pay off the cost of investing in it. Most commonly, this concept is expressed as 'It will pay for itself in X years.'

The most basic measure routinely used is ROI: flexible enough to cope with everything from a one-off direct marketing campaign to a billion pound investment, and providing a powerful basis for measuring one outcome against another, ROI is simple and effective. In fact, many businesses set a target ROI which proposed new ventures must at least match.

At its crudest, suppose we wanted to measure how well a direct mail shot had performed:

Number of pieces mailed	100 000
Cost per piece	2.00
Total mailing cost	200 000
Response rate	1.5%
Number of responses	1500
Sales price	180
Sales revenues	270 000
Revenues less mailing cost	70 000
ROI (net revenues/mailing cost)	35%

To emphasise, this is a crude calculation: it could be refined by, for example, factoring in the operational costs which will have been incurred in processing the sales. Activity-based accounting analysis, which assesses the costs incurred by every activity involved in creating and processing the product, will help give a more accurate measure of profitability at campaign and product level. But, however it is defined, the purpose of the ROI measure is to compute the return generated by a particular marketing investment. It also follows, therefore, that ROI is a very useful tool for comparing the efficiency of different marketing strategies, both at the planning stage, when best estimates will have to be made on outcomes based on results from similar programmes, and after the event, when actuals should be available.

A weakness of ROI is that it is rarely estimated at anything beyond product level: 'This campaign generated these additional sales revenues for this product.' It could be significantly improved by recognising that the marketing activity will have generated new customers who can be cross-sold other products and services. In fact, there is emerging agreement that, where possible, estimates of profitability at product level should be complemented by estimates of profitability at customer level. Customer relationship management (CRM) software aims to do precisely this.

The additional insights which the CRM focus provides are hugely important as marketers can now judge their performance at the level of individual consumers. Conversely, it also allows the performance of customers, so to speak, to be measured, and their value to the business decided. Usually, however, these comparisons can only be carried out once there is a base of live consumers to measure, and a fuller consideration of them is therefore deferred until the chapter on post-launch portfolio management.

It is worth stressing the phrase 'additional insights': enthusiasm for CRM should not lead to an abandonment of product level profitability assessments.

Building a profit and loss account

On the assumption that a financial perspective is needed, a profit and loss account (in the US, income statement or earnings statement) is the basic tool for analysis. Its purpose is simple: to show the income and expenses for the product (or other business unit) for a given period, and thereby identify the profit earned.

The elements

Figure 6.1 is a very simple example which highlights a number of important concepts.

Fees are an important element of the income earned by a financial services product.

Cost of funds is how much the business pays for, in this case, the money it then lends out to its customers: the difference between what it pays and what it charges (its 'net interest margin') is clearly crucial. In this regard, deposit-taking banks are at a considerable advantage over other lenders because they often pay little or nothing by way of interest on amounts held in customers' current (checking) accounts.

	£
Income	
Interest	
Fees	
Total income	
Expenses	
Cost of funds	
Operating costs	
Administrative	
Sales and marketing	
Customer service	
Bad debts written off	
Total expenses	
Net profit before taxes	
Provision for taxes	
Profit after tax	

Figure 6.1 Profit and loss account for the Acme Low Cost Personal Loan

Operating costs can be quite difficult to allocate at product level: usually, some form of analysis based on activity is used. For example, in the Acme Customer Service Centre, one might allocate costs to the Low Cost Personal Loan based on the proportion of all incoming calls which dealt with this product. Alternatively, to reflect the fact that some products are more complicated and generate longer 'talk time', it may be more accurate to establish an average talk time for each of the products serviced by the centre and multiply the number of Low Cost Personal Loan calls by the time it typically takes to deal with them. A similar approach could be used in all the general activities which deal with the product – credit scoring, account set up and so on.

Sales and marketing costs will cover both the costs of acquiring the account in the first place (including any commissions paid to intermediaries, such as brokers or IFAs), and then the continuing cost of communicating with the customer via, for example, statement inserts. These expenses are usually fairly easy to establish on a product by product basis, but if we are selling the Low Cost Personal Loan through a sales force with responsibility for a number of products, some kind of analysis will be called for, probably based on the time a salesperson dedicates to the product over, say, a month. This activity-based approach can be very accurate, but it does require careful and expensive analysis, not just once, but regularly, to ensure that changing conditions are fully reflected.

Bad debt Just as there is room for debate over what is the best activity to use as a basis for allocating cost, so do different organisations take different views on when a debt should be written off as uncollectable, some being more conservative than others. Statutory requirements can also play a part here by defining when a debt can legally be written off.

Attempts to recover past-due amounts, either in-house, or by passing them to specialist debt-collection agencies, can continue after they have been written off. By way of illustration, US experience in 2002 of personal card amounts charged off following bankruptcy was that 1.67 per cent was recovered by a combination of in-house and third party efforts (*The Nilson Report*, February 2003). The accounting treatment and recovery of bad debt is a specialised area, outside the scope of this book.

Forecasting

In the real world, the future is difficult to predict: interest rates can be volatile, stock markets may boom, house prices slump, economies go into recession. These external events will inevitably affect the outcomes we are trying to predict. Under these circumstances, it makes sense to develop forecasts based on the most favourable environment we are likely to experience (usually called the 'best case'), the most difficult we are likely to encounter (the 'worst case'), and the situation somewhere in between these two which is felt to be the 'most likely case'.

'Sensitivity analysis', as this process is known, has two advantages:

1. It compels the forecaster to spell out the assumptions which are being made. Not only is this conducive to accuracy, it also leads to greater care and comprehensiveness in considering market conditions.

2. It makes honesty easier: by legitimising the possibility that things may not go as well as hoped, it reduces the likelihood of undue optimism. Managers responsible for launching new projects are always under some pressure to put the best possible face on things, and the inclusion of a worst case scenario provides a useful corrective.

Sensitivity analysis is not fool-proof: the assumptions can be incomplete, or as a whole unreasonably optimistic or pessimistic. But the requirement to spell them out, together with the underlying rationale, at least brings them to the attention of the decision-maker for approval or rejection.

The terms best case and worst case can need clarification: for instance, in the loyalty rewards scheme mentioned in the table in Figure 6.2, does 'best' mean the highest level of redemption – meaning that customers enrolled in the scheme find it highly motivating and correspondingly expensive to the operator (ignoring the crucial element of incremental sales generated by the programme)? Or does 'best' mean the lowest and correspondingly cheapest level of redemptions – and therefore least interest by customers?

	Best case	Worst case	Most likely
Direct mail response rate using Pack C	1.4%: a similar product to a similar cell generated this level using Pack A	0.4%: a similar product to a similar cell generated this level using Pack B	0.9%: a half way point
Sales of fixed rate mortgage	£300 million, assuming interest rates rising	£150 million, assuming interest rates fall	£200 million, assuming interest rates stable
Loyalty rewards scheme award costs	80% redemption rate (similar programme in other markets)	60% redemption rate (similar programme in other markets)	70% redemption rate (a middle point)
Call centre costs	£2.85 per call, assuming average call length of 1 minute	£8.20 per call, assuming average call length of 3 minutes	£5.50 per call, assuming average call length of 2 minutes

Figure 6.2 Sensitivity analysis

In fact, the likelihood is that there will be several variables for which forecasts have to be made; the table in Figure 6.3 shows how this might work in practice for a mailing featuring an unsecured loan.

Mailing size	1 million								
Pack cost (including postage)	$1								
Mailing cost	$1 million								
Response rate	1%			0.5%			0.75%		
Number of responses	10 000			5000			7500		
Cost per response	$100			$200			$133		
Approval rate	60%	50%	65%	60%	50%	65%	60%	50%	65%
Number of applications approved	6000	5000	6500	3000	2500	3250	4500	3750	4875
Cost per approved loan	$167	$200	$154	$333	$400	$308	$222	$267	$205

Figure 6.3   Forecasting pack performance

The task then is to bring these various scenarios together to determine whether the project meets the criteria – marketing and financial – which have been laid down for it.

Further insights can be gained by trying to assign levels of probability to key variables such as response rate and approval rate: this will help in keeping the range of forecasts realistic.

Another useful concept in thinking about and trying to forecast the elements in a P&L is to classify them according to the table in Figure 6.4.

Element	Description	Example
Decisions	Numbers you can decide	Investment amount
Certainties	Things you know in advance but can't decide	Occupancy costs
Uncertainties	Things you don't know in advance and can't decide	Demand

Source: Dr Sam Savage, *Understanding Uncertainty Through Simulation*, http://analycorp.com/uncertainty/

Figure 6.4   Elements in forecasting

Bringing all these concepts together, we might arrive at a document which looks something like Figure 6.5.

With the rationales and assumptions made clear, a P&L statement of this sort is an important element in the material which a decision-maker will need in reviewing a marketing investment.

	Best case	Worst case	Most likely case
Income			
Interest			
Fees			
Total income			
Expenses			
Operating costs:			
Application review and decisioning			
Account set-up			
Account maintenance			
Documentation issue			
Statementing			
Call centre allowance			
Other administrative			
Sales and marketing:			
Account acquisition			
Communications			
Customer service			
Commissions to third parties			
Financial costs:			
Cost of funds			
Bad debts written off			
Total expenses			
Net profit before taxes			
Provision for taxes			
Profit after tax			
NPV			
ROA			
ROE			

Figure 6.5 Profit and loss account forecasting: the Acme Low Cost Personal Loan

Understanding cash flow

But a P&L account is not the only financial statement which may be called for: if significant inflows and outflows of cash are expected, then a 'cash flow statement' will almost certainly be needed. It is unlikely that a marketer would be asked to develop such a document, but it is an important indicator of financial health, and non-financial specialists should at least be aware of what it does.

Essentially, a cash flow statement sets out, month by month (or weekly or even daily) the amounts of cash the business pays out and receives. If receipts exceed payments, then the business is said to be cash-positive. If it pays out in cash more than it gets in, then it is said to be cash-negative: more important, funds have to be found to support the imbalance. In the cliché, 'cash is king'; and it is not uncommon for a business to be solidly profitable on paper, but to go under, simply because it cannot generate cash sufficient to meet its outgoings.

CASH FLOW STATEMENT
£000s Year 1

Month	1	2	3	4	5	6	7	8	9	10	11	12	Totals
Starting cash	0	2389	1311	919	111	13	90	-442	-252	-118	-712	-457	0
Cash received													
Cash sales	0	650	975	1300	1560	1950	2340	2600	2470	2340	2860	2990	22035
Start up funds	5000	0	0	0	0	0	0	0	0	0	0	0	5000
Total cash receipts	5000	650	975	1300	1560	1950	2340	2600	2470	2340	2860	2990	27035
TOTAL CASH AVAILABLE	5000	3039	2286	2219	1671	1963	2430	2158	2218	2222	2148	2533	27035
Cash paid out													
Cost of sales	0	358	536	715	858	1073	1287	1430	1359	1287	1573	1645	12119
Marketing	1000	750	200	50	50	50	50	50	50	50	50	50	2400
Staff salaries	200	200	200	200	200	200	300	300	300	300	300	300	3000
Other employment expense	30	30	30	30	30	30	45	45	45	45	45	45	450
Telephone	100	100	100	200	200	200	250	250	250	250	250	250	2400
Rent	150	150	150	150	150	150	150	150	150	150	150	150	1800
Utilities	250	0	0	250	0	0	250	0	0	250	0	0	1000
Insurance	100	0	0	100	0	0	100	0	0	100	0	0	400
Professional charges	250	0	0	0	0	0	0	0	0	0	0	0	250
T&E	200	100	100	100	100	100	100	100	100	150	150	150	1450
Property taxes	200	0	0	200	0	0	200	0	0	200	0	0	800
Property maintenance	20	20	20	20	20	20	20	20	20	20	20	20	240
Postage	30	10	10	15	15	15	20	20	20	20	20	25	220
Office supplies	50	0	0	50	0	0	60	0	0	70	0	0	230
Interest on start-up funds	21	21	21	21	21	21	21	21	21	21	21	21	250
Other	10	10	10	15	15	15	20	20	20	20	20	20	195
TOTAL CASH PAID OUT	2611	1748	1377	2116	1659	1873	2873	2406	2334	2933	2599	2675	27204
NET CASH FLOW	2389	1291	909	104	12	90	-443	-248	-116	-711	-451	-142	-169
Interest receivable/(payable)	0	20	11	8	1	0	1	-4	-2	-1	-6	-4	24
ENDING CASH	2389	1311	919	111	13	90	-442	-252	-118	-712	-457	-146	-146

Assumes supplier invoices paid on receipt

Figure 6.6 Cash flow statement: simple example

In the simple example shown in Figure 6.6, even with start-up funds of £5 million, the business begins to be cash-negative from month 7, although towards the end of the year the signs are that growing sales are pegging back the overdraft. From a management point of view, either sales revenues will have to increase, or expenses will have to be cut. Providing more start up capital is not the answer: this simply drives up interest payments – and note that there is no provision for repayment of the principal (or annual staff bonuses, for that matter). Clearly, it will be crucial to extend the forecast, certainly into Year 2 and probably into Year 3, to see whether the business will move into cash-positive territory. Beyond a three year time horizon, few forecasts are worth making.

The American Express Revenue Statement and Expenses Statement shown in Figures 6.7 and 6.8 illustrate many of the points made so far.

American Express Consolidated Revenues $bn			
Year ending 31 December	*2002*	*2001*	*2000*
Discount revenue	7931	7714	7779
Interest and dividends, net	2991	2137	3290
Management and distribution fees	2285	2458	2812
Securitisation income	1941	1432	1012
Net card fees	1726	1675	1651
Cardmember lending net finance charge revenue	1485	1424	1255
Travel commissions and fees	1408	1537	1821
Other commissions and fees	2113	2088	1989
Life and other insurance revenues	802	674	575
Other	1125	1443	1491
Total	**25 807**	**22 582**	**23 675**

Figure 6.7 American Express Revenue Statement

Explanatory notes to the Revenue Statement

Discount revenue: discounts received on cardmembers' charges at merchants
Interest and dividends, net: from securities and loans
Management and distribution fees: collected from American Express proprietary mutual funds and other American Express proprietary assets under American Express management
Securitisation income: revenue associated with retained and subordinated interests in securitised loans, servicing income from loans sold and gains received at the time of securitisation
Net card fees: net of refunds
Cardmember lending net finance charge revenue: net of interest expense
Other: fees from financial planning, consulting and business services and miscellaneous investment income.

Note that in Figure 6.8 marketing and promotion costs are roughly similar to occupancy and equipment, and that by far the single biggest cost is people.

| American Express Expenses $bn | | | |
Year ending 31 December	2002	2001	2000
Human resources	5725	6271	6633
Provisions for losses and benefits:			
Annuities and investment certificates	1217	1318	1355
Life insurance, international banking and other	1040	909	694
Charge card	960	1195	1006
Cardmember lending	1369	1318	891
Professional services	2021	1651	1530
Marketing and promotion	1548	1301	1515
Occupancy and equipment	1458	1574	1528
Interest	1082	1501	1354
Communications	514	528	514
Restructuring charge	(7)	605	–
Disaster recovery charge	(7)	90	–
Other	3160	2725	2747
Total	**20 080**	**20 986**	**19 767**
Pretax income	3727	1596	3908
Income tax provision	1056	285	1098
Net income after tax	**2671**	**1311**	**2810**

Figure 6.8 American Express Expenses Statement

MARKETING MEASURES

Marketers have also developed performance measures with (more or less) agreed definitions. Among the most commonly found in the financial services industry are:

Market share

This is the proportion of the market (however defined) estimated to be held by the product in terms of sales by unit and/or value.

Share of wallet

This measure recognises that 'share of market' relies on a particular set of assumptions about what constitutes the market. 'Share of wallet' extends the share of market concept by relating to decisions made at individual consumer level. To illustrate, a personal credit card product may have:

- 30 per cent of market share as expressed as a percentage of the number of all personal credit card accounts in the market.

- 35 per cent of outstanding balances as expressed as a percentage of outstanding balances on all personal credit card accounts in the market.

- 12 per cent of all payment transactions by number made by the consumers actually holding this card.

- 25 per cent of all payment transactions by value made by the consumers actually holding this card.

Whereas the first two are measures of market share, the second two are measures of share of wallet: they measure what proportion of payment transactions its customers choose to use the card for. The value of the share of wallet concept is its recognition that, for payment cards, the competition is not just other cards, but other methods of payment – cheques, cash, electronic funds transfer and so on. Accordingly, success for this card may well be measured by how often consumers select it rather than cash or cheques to settle a transaction.

Similarly, a bank may measure the sales success of its in-house unit trusts first by their overall market share as compared with competing unit trusts, then by the share they have gained among those of the bank's customer base who have bought savings products from it. Clearly, market share and share of wallet are measuring different but complementary things.

HYBRID MARKETING/FINANCIAL MEASURES

The distinction between financial and marketing measures is really an artefact created by arbitrary ideas about where one discipline ends and another begins. Performance criteria are now being developed which combine elements of both approaches. Perhaps the best known is:

Customer lifetime value   The measures we have discussed so far are product-based: they attempt to gauge how well the product is performing. A different and equally valuable dimension comes if we try to measure how valuable the customer is to us. By calculating all the revenues generated by a customer over the entire period that they do business with us, less the costs associated with recruiting and servicing them, lifetime value (LTV) provides a very useful tool for segmenting the customer base. Figure 6.9 illustrates a simple example.

One of the advantages of LTV is that it shows very clearly the value of customer loyalty: once the recruitment cost has been recovered, the customer who continues to do business with us is much more profitable than one who defects. It also suggests that, simply by increasing the amount of additional products and services which they buy, customers can become even more profitable. And who is more likely to buy additional products than the loyal customer?

LTV analysis essentially regards the customer as being an income stream over time. Taking this to its logical conclusion, it would make sense to calculate the net

	Year 1	Year 2	Year 3	Year 4	Year 5
Recruitment cost	150	Nil	Nil	Nil	Nil
Annual servicing costs	40	40	40	40	40
Total costs	190	40	40	40	40
Income	120	120	120	120	120
Annual value	(70)	80	80	80	80
LTV	(70)	10	90	170	250

Figure 6.9 Lifetime value

present value of the LTV income stream. The effect of time could also be reflected in the cost and income elements.

In some ways, attempting to calculate LTV before the product has even been launched is clearly a little premature: nevertheless, by stressing the long-term nature of the relationship we hope to build with our customers, it has a value which makes the exercise worthwhile.

So which of these measures, financial, marketing or hybrid, should we use when assembling our business plan? Possibly the most useful would be PTI, ROA, and market share: together, they give us an estimate of how much profit the business will make, how well that profit relates to the assets necessary to generate it, and how we plan to perform relative to the competition. Measuring how well the product performs at consumer level is perhaps best left to wait until we actually have some consumers – although it might be interesting to set provisional targets for market share (macro level) and share of wallet (micro level).

PICKING A TIME SCALE

After 'How do we measure how well we are doing?' perhaps the next question to answer is 'Over what time frame?'

As John Maynard Keynes pointed out, 'In the long run, we are all dead', and there is usually little practical point in attempting to forecast outcomes more than five years ahead. In fact, when the effect of events in an increasingly inter-dependent world can travel around it in a nanosecond, some would say that even three years is ambitious. Nevertheless, convention usually calls for a planning horizon of five years, although realists may not attach a great deal of weight to the projections for Years 4 and 5. Phrases such as short term and medium term are meaningless without definition.

However, some key forecasts deal with a time scale of months or even weeks rather than years. Examples would include measures of:

- sales

- the effect of advertising campaigns (changes in brand recognition, for instance)

- response to direct marketing (applications received, website hits, 0800 calls received, coupons returned)

- expense budgets

- cash flow.

SUMMING UP

All organisations have to justify their existence. In a competitive world, those which use scarce assets (scarce in the economist's sense, that there is more than one use to which they can be put) have to demonstrate that they can generate a better return from those assets than an alternative use. While there is a good deal of scope for controversy in other fields about what measures which should be used (or even, in some cases, whether the organisation actually has measurable outputs and inputs), at least in the financial services industry there are generally accepted yardsticks for gauging both fiscal and marketing performance. Measures such as market share, PTI, ROI and NPV have widely accepted definitions within companies, between companies, and even across national borders. Just as important as measuring profitability at account level is measuring profitability at customer level: together, the two approaches provide a balanced way of assessing performance.

CHAPTER 7

Communication and Distribution

INTRODUCTION

In many industries, the tasks of communicating the product to its target audience and then getting it into consumers' hands are quite separate: motor vehicles, food and drink, household appliances and photographic equipment are just a few examples of products which are principally marketed by their manufacturers, but distributed by retailers. Of course, the retailers may also promote these products themselves, but the strong likelihood is that much of this activity will be paid for by the manufacturer. Hybrids do exist; for example, in the UK around 35 per cent of filling stations are operated by the oil companies themselves, the remainder being independently owned. Even so, it is the oil company which does the advertising.

In the financial services industry, probably the majority of services by value are both marketed and distributed by the 'manufacturer', although this varies by type: banking products, for example, are almost exclusively distributed and marketed by banks, insurance products have traditionally relied on a mix of intermediaries and in-house sales (though banking networks play an ever more important role) while mortgages are increasingly being distributed by specialist brokers.

Nevertheless, even though the same organisation may be responsible for both communication and distribution, the two tasks are quite different: communication essentially deals with informing potential customers about the product in such a way as to arouse their interest, and prompt them to take some action – probably making an enquiry, or filling in an application. Distribution is about getting the product into the customer's hands; in the special case of the financial services industry, it may well also include some element of screening, credit checking, mandatory two-way information disclosure, and cooling-off periods.

Many channels are available for communication and distribution. Some, such as direct mail, branch networks, the Internet and direct selling are particularly relevant to the financial services industry: they are discussed in some detail. The chapter provides an overview of the strengths and weaknesses of the others.

Generally, it aims to answer the questions:

- What are the choices in communication and distribution?
- What are their strengths and weaknesses?
- How do I make the choices?

COMMUNICATION: THE THEORY

Psychologists have a long-standing interest in consumer behaviour and have undertaken a good deal of research into how we respond to advertising messages, and how that response translates into buying decisions. Proposed as long ago as 1925 in the book *The Psychology of Selling and Advertising* by E. K. Strong, the venerable AIDA model has the appeal of simplicity and intuitive rightness in explaining customer buying behaviour; although it has been supplemented by more complex notions of cognition, it still is a powerful and practical tool for organising any selling communication. The acronym AIDA stands for Awareness, Interest, Desire and Action, as shown in Figure 7.1.

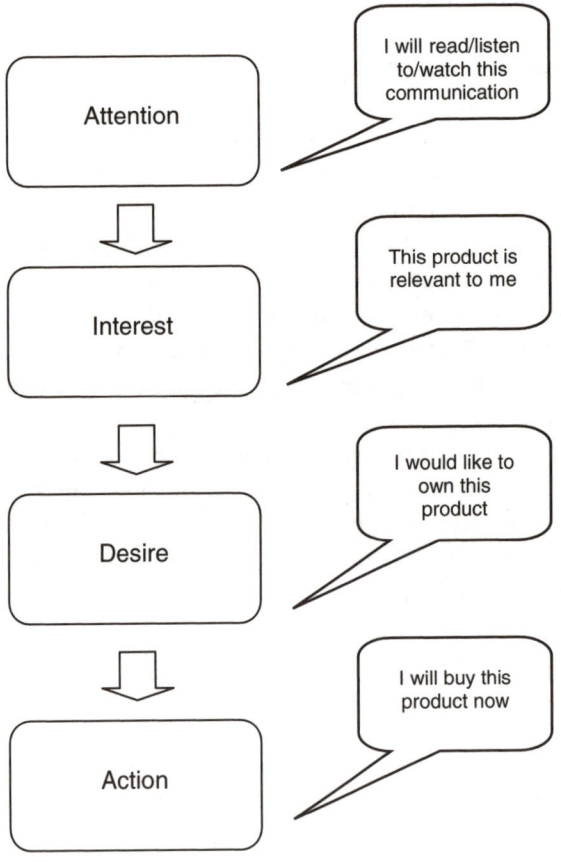

Figure 7.1   AIDA model

Perhaps the most important overlays on the AIDA model are those which recognise the individuality of the consumer. Various refinements have been suggested, of which the following may be singled out:

Affordability: Can I afford to buy this?

Salience: How important is this to me just now?

Tastes and preferences: Is this the sort of thing I buy?

These filters are in operation at each stage of the communication and buying process (see Figure 7.2).

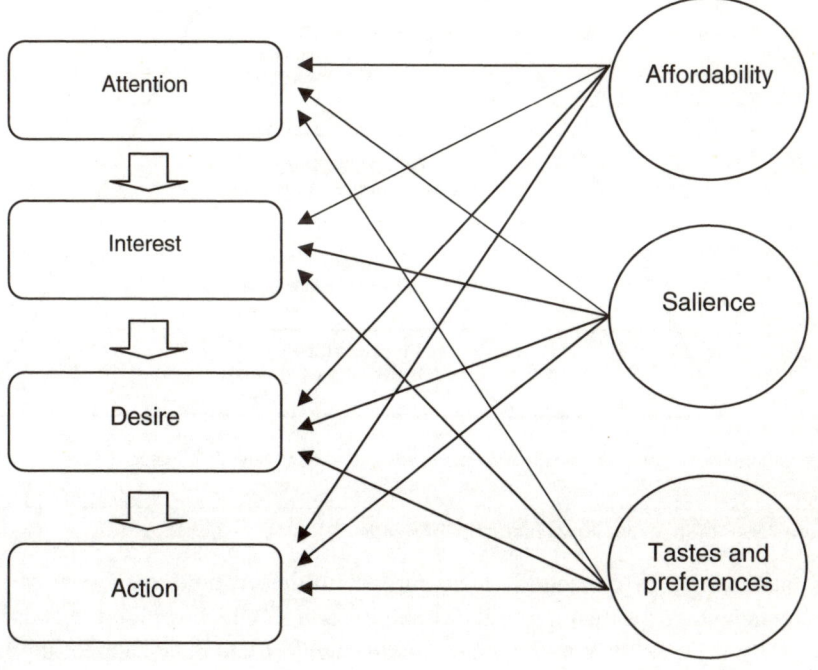

Figure 7.2 Suggested refinements of the AIDA model

In developing communications materials, it is important to bear in mind the complex interplay of these factors. For example, life insurance for young people is cheap (affordability), but is rarely top of mind (salience), and is not 'the kind of thing people like me spend a lot of time thinking about' (tastes and preferences). Campaigns aimed at this market will therefore have to work hard just to get the attention of potential customers.

Advertisers in the financial services industry also have to contend with the difficulty that what they are selling is not usually of itself very interesting, attractive or easy to understand. At best, purchase is usually on the precautionary principle and, often enough, actively begrudged. In terms of Maslow's famous pyramid of needs, financial services purchases are usually second level, that is to say, they are expected to provide some level of security.

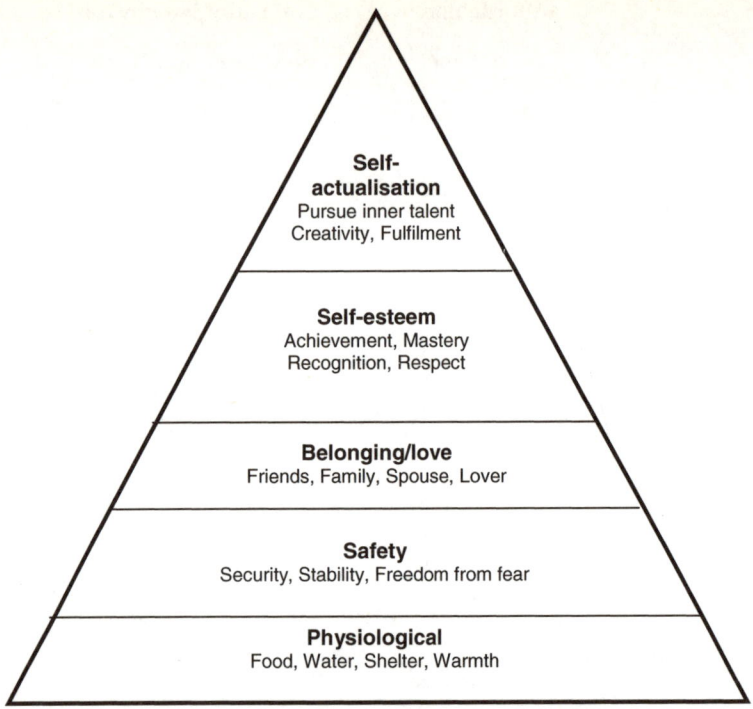

Source: Maslow, A. (1970) *Motivation and Personality* (2nd edition). New York: Harper & Row

Figure 7.3   Abraham Maslow's hierarchy of needs

Interestingly, by moving the focus further up the pyramid, marketers can very much strengthen the customer relationship: products which respond effectively to our strongest inner drives for belonging and recognition can build great loyalty. In the financial services industry, examples of this approach would include the carefully personalised services of Coutts Bank, and the American Express 'Says more about you than cash ever can' campaigns.

These overlays to AIDA all revolve around the recognition that customers are individuals – that they bring to the buying process their own unique needs, expectations, experiences and cultural make-up. Outside the face-to-face selling environment, however, the large scale of most media make it impossible to deal in individualised communications. As a first approximation, a good deal of effort is therefore devoted by research groups into identifying groups of individual customers who behave similarly. Often given fanciful names ('merchant venturers', 'fearful planners' and the like), the most important requirement for these groups is that they be big enough to be worth communicating with, and have sufficient characteristics in common for them to be identifiable. Accordingly, 'merchant venturers' might be described as having 'entrepreneurial risk-taking behaviour' – implying that they may well be good prospects for high risk, high return investments – and categorised as between 35 and 50, with graduate level education, overwhelmingly male, and living in higher-grade residential areas. On this basis, it would be possible either to buy in lists of consumers with these characteristics, and/or to review our own client database to identify existing customers who meet this description.

COMMUNICATION: THE PRACTICE

Taking all of these factors together, financial advertisers have a distinctly more difficult task in reaching and persuading their customers than, say, drinks marketers. In fact, cutting through the clutter of messages which clamours for any consumer's attention calls for maximum impact.

DECIDING THE MESSAGE

Take, for instance, the magazine insert in Figure 7.4.

Figure 7.4 Alliance and Leicester magazine insert.

So important was the interest rate felt to be that, not content using a massive display of it, to make sure of getting the reader's attention the display was repeated. This treatment is so dominating that the only elements it leaves room for are what the product is, a 'call to action', and the advertiser's logo.

Clearly, other approaches could have been used: for instance rather than focus so single-mindedly on the rate of interest, the advertiser could have majored on products and services which could have been bought with the loan. Opinions can differ sharply on the creative approach to be used, but there are some rules of thumb which can help the decision-making process:

- Simple usually works better than complicated: this clearly was in the minds of the Alliance and Leicester marketing team.

- Are the tone of voice (authoritative through to friendly) and language (formal through to 'street') appropriate for the audience, the product and the advertiser?

- What do we want the audience to do or think or feel as a result of receiving the message?

Testing the emerging options with focus groups can also provide some guidance.

As well as these considerations, there are important externally imposed constraints on what can be included in a marketing communication: apart from the need to be legal, decent, honest and truthful which applies to all advertisers, the financial services industry has to meet special statutory requirements. What these are, and what bodies are responsible for implementing them, will vary from market to market. In the UK, for example, the Financial Services Authority is the independent body charged with regulating the industry. But regulations now reach across borders: the European Union is committed to developing requirements which will affect all its members. An example is the requirement for institutions advertising investment funds to show standardised fund performance data, rather than selecting a period which shows the fund's results in the best light.

Returning to the Alliance and Leicester flyer, it certainly responds to the attention, affordability and action components of the modified AIDA model; but what about the other elements – interest, desire, salience, tastes and preferences? To answer that, we have to look at the publication in which the flyer was inserted: an upscale homes and gardens magazine. This opens up the whole question of media selection.

CHOOSING THE RIGHT COMMUNICATION MEDIUM

We saw earlier that all consumers are different and that advertising communications must reflect that complexity.

But that same complexity is also reflected in the media from which our consumers can choose: in other words, there is almost certainly some combination of media which either singly, or in combination with others, allows us to reach the targeted customer more effectively (see Figure 7.5).

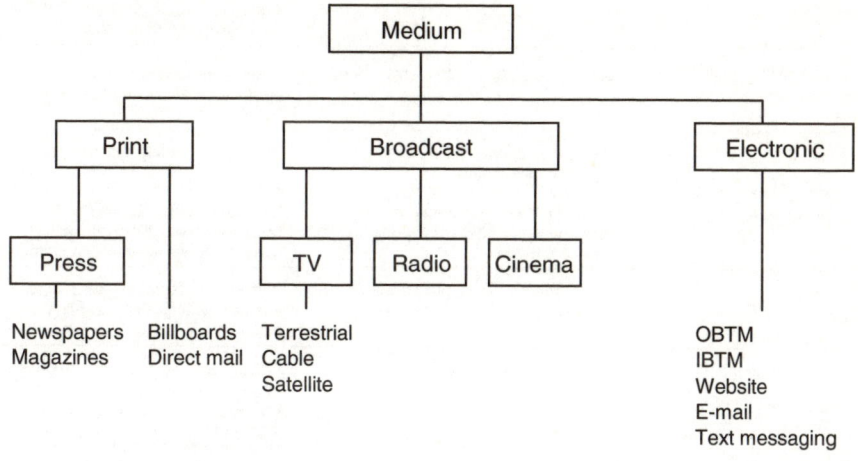

Figure 7.5 Communications media

It is precisely this which has driven the proliferation of special interest media (magazines and websites) as publishers rush to identify and meet the needs of emerging interest groups. This works in the financial services industry as well: there are specialist publications for borrowers and investors, just as there are for sailors and joggers.

Additionally, there are more general interest publications which reach consumers who may have particular potential: in the case of the flyer, the advertiser probably chose a home improvements publication because many of its readers could be interested in taking out a personal loan. There are even mass market publications which have built up a particular market place for financial services, both in their usual pages, and in regular financial supplements. Although these examples are taken from the press, exactly the same arguments apply to all the other media: in the case of TV, for example, it is possible to buy advertising slots during particular programmes: the principal news bulletin is often chosen for financial advertising. To help the selection process, all advertising media have sales departments which can provide detailed audience and readership research.

The essential point being made here is that media choice is crucial in reaching our target market cost-effectively.

The table in Figure 7.6 gives a very general overview of the strengths and weaknesses of the main communication media. It is followed by a discussion of the options most often used today by the financial services industry and those channels which are now emerging: press, TV, direct mail, telemarketing, the Internet, e-mail and text messaging.

Medium	Advantages	Disadvantages
Internet	Quick; can be linked to appropriate third party sites	Only reaches Internet-enabled households; some indication of higher-risk applicants for loans; except for simple products, better at communication than fulfilment
SMS text messaging	Quick, cheap, (currently) rarity value	Short messages only, low production values (though this may improve)
E-mail	Quick, very cheap, production quality improving all the time	Possibly terminally tainted by spam
Direct mail	Extremely flexible in terms of size, target, testing and creativity. Highly measurable	Low (and falling) response rates in mature markets. Efficient mail service not available in all countries
Radio	Fast response times; production cheap	With some exceptions, audiences relatively young. Poor at giving detail
TV (including DRTV)	High impact, big audiences; some selectivity in audience type	Audiences in slow decline. Anything beyond the most basic commercial very expensive and time consuming to produce; air-time expensive
Cinema	High impact, strong production values	Young audiences, poor at detail, long lead times for production
Press • Newspapers • Magazines	Production inexpensive and fast. Good for detail • Readerships big (nationals) or local (locals) • Highly segmented audiences • Much better reproduction values than newspapers	• Readerships in slow decline • More expensive and longer lead times than newspapers
Outdoor	High impact, good attention getter	Poor at giving detail
Sales force • In house • Independent	• Can be highly committed and well trained • Flexibility to cope with overload; no fixed overheads	• Expensive • Not always easy to control
Intermediaries	Payment usually by results; no fixed overheads	Not always easy to control
Telemarketing • Outbound • Inbound	• Gets fast responses • Good for generating leads • Product can be tailored to subject of inbound call • Hit rates can be relatively high	• Unpopular – seen as intrusive • Not suited to complex products • Proper balance between sales and service important • Good customer service staff not always good salespeople
POS/POP (US)	Good at getting attention; can be cheap	Distribution can be expensive; not good at providing detail
PR	Good at getting attention; can be selective and cheap	A scene setter only; difficult to measure results

Figure 7.6 Strengths and weaknesses of communications media

PRESS

Although, in the UK at least, readership of national dailies is in slow decline, they still reach large audiences – larger in this country, in fact, than most other industrialised nations.

	Adults (15+)	Men	% of total	Women	% of total
	Monday to Saturday average issues, 000s				
Sun	9380	5338	57%	4041	43%
Daily Mail	5919	2937	50%	2982	50%
Daily Mirror	5378	2846	53%	2532	47%
Daily Telegraph	2386	1318	55%	1068	45%
Daily Express	2193	1161	53%	1032	47%
Daily Star	1885	1398	74%	487	26%
Times	1867	1097	59%	770	41%
Daily Record	1517	807	53%	710	47%
Metro	1469	872	59%	596	41%
Guardian	1348	769	57%	579	43%
Evening Standard (London)	1061	627	59%	434	41%
Independent	582	345	59%	237	41%
Financial Times	546	398	73%	148	27%

Source: National Readership Survey, April 2002 – March 2003

Figure 7.7 Readership of daily newspapers

The table in Figure 7.7 is based on readership, rather than circulation. It shows, for example, that unlike other titles *Daily Mail* readers are almost equally balanced between men and women. But there is a great gap of both numbers and audience type between the so-called red-tops (tabloids with red mast-heads, mostly aimed at C2DE men (skilled manual, semi-skilled and unskilled)) and the broadsheets, which aim at a more upscale readership. Highly detailed readership analyses are available, both from the media themselves and national surveys such as the NRS.

Because individual titles aim, to a greater or lesser extent, at differentiated audiences, there is also some ability to select particular groups of readers. Ad production costs are also usually relatively low, and lead times usually short, except for the most successful monthly magazines. Importantly, a press ad can provide a very great amount of detail about the product. For all these reasons, the financial services industry continues to make heavy use of the national press in particular, both for attention getting and lead generation. Local press also gets a proportion of some advertisers' budgets, but it can offer poorer value than the nationals in terms of cost per thousand readers who see the ad.

The strength of magazines is their ability to reach very sharply selected and even very small audiences: there are very few socio-economic segments or interest groups which do not have a magazine publication aimed squarely at them. This ability to deliver to selected audiences makes them a very valuable option for the marketer:

mortgages, savings products, car buyers, finance directors, students, retired people – all have magazines dedicated to them.

In fact, for advertisers in both dailies and magazines the challenge is how to cut through the welter of competing ads. One solution is to insert a flyer: although more expensive, inserts often generate higher readership levels than conventional ads in the same issue. Unfortunately, media owners are very well aware of this, and some magazines in particular are notorious for the number of inserts they are willing to take. The maximum I have found is nine inserts in one issue – presumably the maximum that the publishers' production machinery will allow. Others are more circumspect.

The most common measures of press advertising's theoretical effectiveness are reach (what proportion of a given audience will see the ad) and frequency (how often they will see it). But this only estimates the potential readership for the campaign: a better test of effectiveness is to research how many readers actually saw the ad, and what they remember of it.

TV

In many markets, TV's ability to deliver mass audiences is declining, as the traditional national broadcast stations are supplemented by satellite and/or cable channels. Just as with magazines, these latter make a very conscious attempt to appeal to particular audiences, although the economics of TV production make it more difficult than it is for print media to reach micro audiences with quality output.

Nevertheless, few financial advertisers wishing to reach large audiences will ignore the impact and reach which TV offers. By careful selection of programme, they can also differentiate to some extent between target groups. It would make sense, for example, to advertise personal loans during programmes dealing with home improvements. A weakness of TV is its inability to handle complexity, and it is therefore best used as an attention getter and scene setter, especially if combined with a website address or free/reduced rate phone number to generate leads.

TV advertising is usually sold on the basis of what combination of spots and placement will buy a given result. For example, a TV campaign might be designed so that 40 per cent of all housewives see it four times. In the jargon, this would be described as a housewife TVR (television rating) of 40 with an OTS (opportunities to see) of 4.

More generally, the weight of a cross-media campaign is often measured in gross ratings points (GRPs). GRP is usually defined as reach (against a target audience) multiplied by average frequency. For example, if a campaign reached 80 per cent of men aged 25 to 39 earning £20 000 or more and they saw it on average 4 times, it would be said to have a GRP against this audience of 320.

DIRECT MAIL

A fascinating compound of art and science, direct mail (DM) is so heavily used by the financial services industry that it has to be singled out for special mention. However, this is a specialised world, and there is space here only to mention some of its most important features.

Direct Mail and Credit Card Marketing in the US

- In 2001, around 33 million credit card applications were produced in the US from slightly more than 5 billion direct mail solicitations – a response rate of 0.7%.
  CardFlash 11 April, 2002

- A study by Vertis has found that 48% of consumers said they learned about a credit card company via direct mail. Other sources include friend or relative (7%), at their bank (7%), special event/in-person promotion (4%), Internet (3%), or telemarketer (3%).
  CardFlash 16 August, 2002

- Direct mail credit card offers

Period	Mail Volume in millions	Response Rates
3Q/01	1174.0	0.6%
2Q/01	1265.4	0.4%
1Q/01	1208.3	0.7%
4Q/00	1033.8	0.8%
3Q/00	888.0	0.6%
2Q/00	991.8	0.4%
1Q/00	629.4	0.7%
4Q/99	510.2	0.7%
3Q/99	710.3	0.9%

Source: BAIGlobal, Inc. quoted in *CardFlash* 14 January 2002.

At the heart of DM lies the discipline of testing. The idea here is to compare the pulling power of different creative approaches by mailing each to a different group or cell; to reduce the effect of variables other than the mailing on the results, the cells are set up to be as similar as possible. Whichever package does best becomes the champion (also known as 'control'), which subsequent new approaches will challenge. 'Best', of course, requires definition: depending on context, in increasing order of precision, 'best' could mean:

- highest response rate
- lowest cost response
- lowest cost approved application.

Note that these definitions measure different things: for example, the pack which pulls the highest overall response may not generate the lowest cost per approved application. In such a case, a commercial balance would have to be struck between a high number of responses, many of which fail at application review stage, and a low number of high quality responses.

Whichever measure is chosen as being most appropriate for the product, the direct mail agency – and it is essential to work with a group with extensive experience in direct mail, and ideally also in financial services – should be briefed to create a number of different test packages. The exact number will depend on the scale of the marketing operation, but there should be enough to test a range of different approaches without there being so many that it is difficult to compare results, or that the mailing cells become too small to get reliable results.

Testing is not confined to creative approaches: it can also be used to assess the responsiveness of different lists or cells, different product propositions, pricing strategies and most other relevant variables. The key is to ensure that outcomes are actionable: there

---

Improving Results

According to a survey commissioned by Vertis, just over one-third of adults (34%) said that they had responded to direct mail advertising in the past 30 days (either by mail, telephone, in person, or through a website) in the US in 2001.

By 2003 this figure had increased to nearly half (46%). Moreover, the Younger Baby Boomer generation's response rates had risen most significantly, from 36% to 49%.

Weekly reading
The year-to-year figures for weekly readership of direct mail proved remarkably consistent, remaining at a level 55%. However, weekly direct mail readership was growing most significantly among adults with a household income of US$75 000 or more (rising to 59% in 2003, up from 53% in 2002).

Almost three-quarters (74%) of the adults surveyed confirmed that they read direct mail, in line with 2002's total of 73%. Seniors and adults aged 35–44 represented the biggest percentage increases over the previous year, rising from 65% to 75% (for the seniors) and from 73% to 78% (for those aged 35–44).

Life insurance success
The survey found that direct life insurance industries were particularly successful in their direct mail communications over the previous two years. Respondents proved to be 6% more likely to purchase life insurance directly as a result of direct mail, telephone calls, or the Internet, without seeing an agent (46% in 2003, up from 40% in 2001).

Source: Wise Marketer Thursday 19 June, 2003.

is little point in establishing beyond doubt that left-handed redheads over 45 respond to the offer better than any other group if you cannot acquire lists of left-handed redheads over 45. It is also usually best to test only one variable at a time, although the statistical technique of multi-variate analysis does make it possible, with careful design, to test a number of variables simultaneously, to see which combination is the most effective.

The fundamental flexibility and precise measurability of DM are what set it apart from the traditional broadcast and print media.

The examples of direct mail material in Figures 7.8 and 7.9 show the AIDA principle in action.

Note a very conservative use by Egg of the outer envelope (OE): the face of the OE carries an anodyne and unspecific phrase, which relies for any effect it might have on the recipient reading the reverse.

Compare this with a much bolder approach from the Halifax in Figure 7.10, which not only spells out clearly and interestingly its main message, but uses the reverse to add urgency to the call to action.

TELEMARKETING

The crash of outbound telemarketing (OBTM) looks likely to be almost as spectacular as its rise: as one of the leading US operators commented ruefully, 'We have very nearly killed the goose that laid the golden eggs.' Overuse of what is a uniquely intrusive medium, allied with dubious practices in some parts of the industry, have led to increasing customer resistance, culminating in the introduction of mandatory 'Do not call' lists in many jurisdictions. As a result, MBNA which in 2002 generated approximately 34 per cent of its new credit card accounts in the USA through 16 telemarketing facilities in 10 states, is expecting to see its reliance on this source diminish sharply. The company quoted 'Changing consumer attitudes and federal and state regulatory initiatives such as do-not-call lists' as the reasons for the change. (*CardFlash*, 1 April 2003). Other financial services institutions report similar experiences: at Citigroup, for example, two-thirds of the products it sold to cardholders in 1999 came through outbound calls made by telemarketers; today, less than a third do (*Dow Jones*, 28 January 2003).

Validating issuers' nervousness was the response in the US to the Federal Trade Commission's introduction of the 'Do Not Call' Register: on 27 June 2003, the day the service was launched, 7 million telephone numbers were logged into the system, and by 1 July, nearly 14 million telephone numbers had been registered. The weight and quality of the response (85 per cent of the registrations were made online) led the FTC to forecast that 60 million phone numbers could be registered within the first 12 months (*CardFlash*, 1 July 2003). Other countries are known to be studying this US initiative closely, with a view to introducing it within the next few years.

Added to growing consumer resistance to OBTM are:

- the difficulties of selling a complex product in an unsolicited phone call

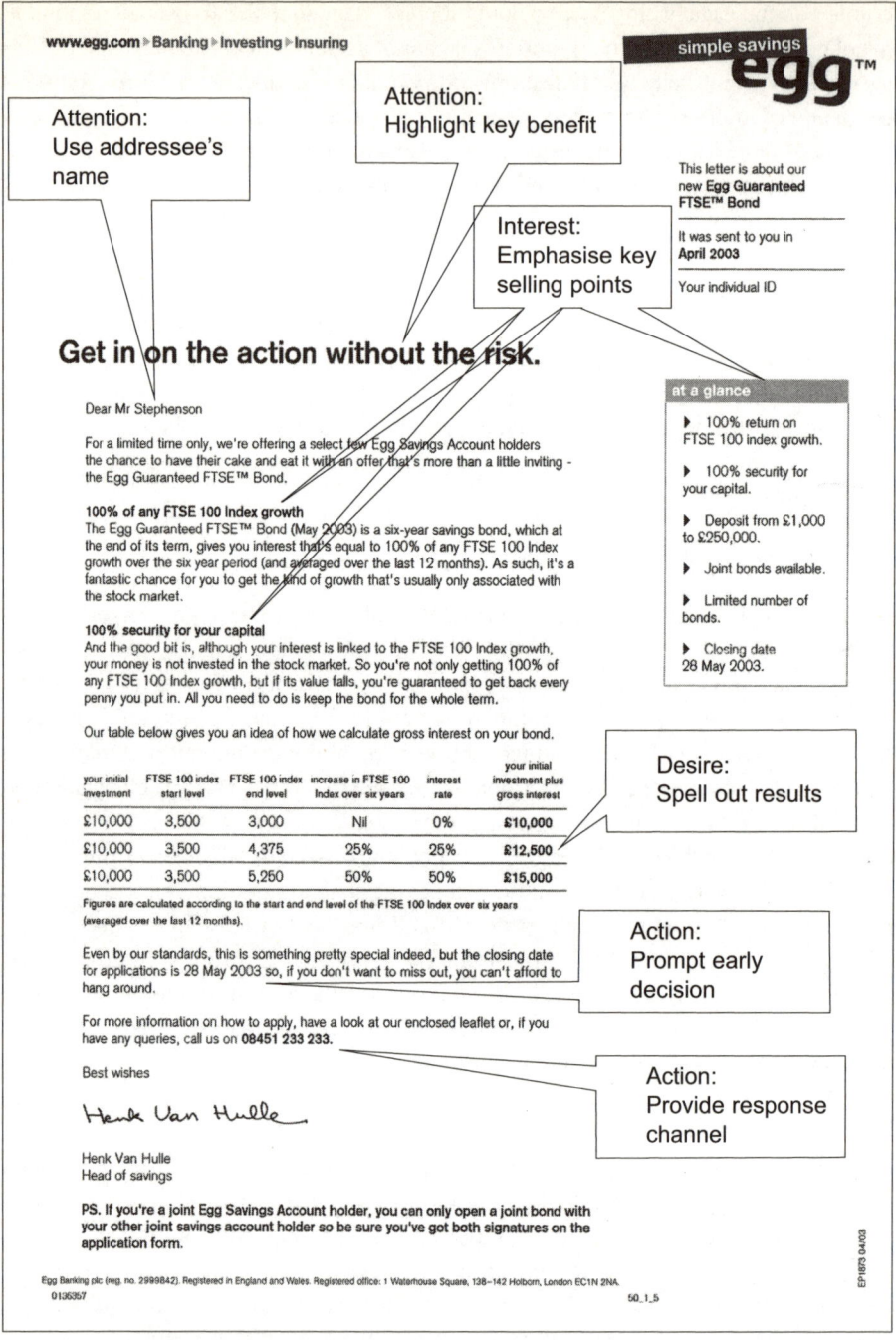

Figure 7.8 AIDA in action: Egg banking letter. Reproduced with permission of Egg

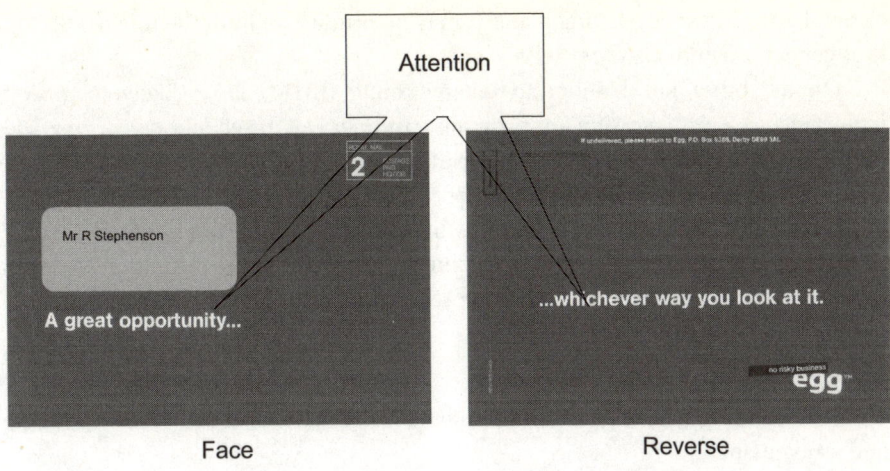

Figure 7.9   AIDA in action: Egg banking direct mail envelope. Reproduced with permission of Egg

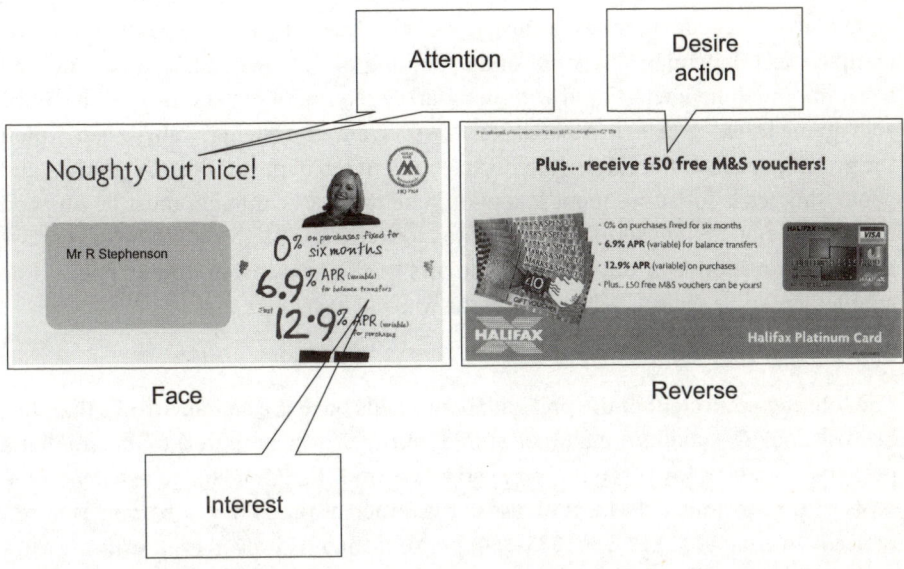

Figure 7.10   AIDA in action: Halifax direct mail envelope. Reproduced with permission of Halifax

(note that MBNA, which had been very successful with OBTM, specialises in affinity group marketing, so that its products are likely to get a more sympathetic response than others);

- a mandatory 'cooling-off' period following initial consumer agreement, which results in high drop out rates in many cases.

Generally, for future marketing plans, it may be prudent to limit the role of OBTM to lead generation and customer service calls.

On the other hand, inbound telemarketing (IBTM) looks likely to grow in importance as a way of using an incoming customer call to sell add-ons or upgrades. Citigroup's experience is interesting: the average length of a call that does not include an additional sales offer is about three minutes. With the offer, the call lengthens by about 30 to 40 seconds. But the added cost is worthwhile; about one out of five products offered to a customer is purchased (*Dow Jones*, 28 January 2003). With other institutions reporting a 15 per cent hit rate, IBTM is a communications medium with substantial potential.

THE INTERNET

The Internet offers a number of communication channels, each with its own strengths and weaknesses.

The website

Many industries can both communicate and distribute their products electronically; apart from simple lending and insurance products, to which a website is very well suited, the financial services industry cannot. Many financial products are too complex, too dependent on a full understanding of the customer's needs and, not least, too much hedged around with mandatory requirements and procedures to be sold on the Internet. Even in these cases, however, a well-designed website can exploit the growing reach of the Internet to do an excellent job of promoting the product and generating leads for subsequent follow-up. The emphasis, though, must be on good design: it is not enough simply to design an attractive site – it must also be easy to use and fast to respond. In other words, the arts of the advertising agency need to be supplemented by the specialist skills of the website developer.

Banner advertising

The Internet equivalent of the press ad, banner ads have the characteristics that they can use cookies (small programmes stored on the user's computer) to ensure that a particular reader doesn't see the same ad twice, and that they charge usually on the basis of impressions (CPM – the cost per number of times that a banner is seen), typically in a range of £15–£30 ($25–$50) per thousand. However, even with the extra creative impetus of ads using software such as Macromedia Flash, 'click-through rates' are dropping all the time, often to well below 1 per cent, so that the cost per click (CPC – cost per request to view a website page) that an ad generates can rise very steeply.

As with any form of advertising, the key to effective Internet banner ads is careful selection of the sites to ensure their relevance to the target audience.

Sponsored links

This precision in reaching interested consumers is exactly the advantage claimed for the sponsored links which appear on the pages of results displayed by search engines.

For example, if an Internet user requests material on investment trusts, a series of ads from investment trust companies will be shown alongside the results. This form of advertising is growing very rapidly. Advertisers pay per click, currently around 23 pence (37 cents) on average (*The Economist*, 19 July 2003).

Pop-up ads

This communication device labours under the dual handicaps of being less precise in its targeting than sponsored links, and annoying to the user. Misuse by a minority of advertisers has led to third party pop-ups being banned by many major portals, and the wide availability of free software which intercepts them before they reach the user. Consequently, the future of pop-ups appears to be in doubt, at least for reputable advertisers on sites other than their own.

E-mail

Abuse of this channel by 'spam' mailers is a major problem, not least for legitimate marketers. But a 2002 study in the US by Synergistics Research uncovered some cause for optimism: it found that two-thirds of Internet users report receiving e-mails promoting financial accounts and services – typically about ten a week – and crucially, one-fifth of these respondents say that they have actually obtained a financial service as a result. Other US e-mail research has shown that, as a marketing channel, e-mail currently produces about 3 per cent of all new credit card accounts (*CardFlash*, 26 September 2002). Among permission-based e-mails, in the US those from financial services vendors were more likely to be opened than those from other industries (48 per cent), but they also registered the lowest click-through rates (5.8 per cent) (*DoubleClick*, quoted in *CardFlash*, 28 August 2003). These findings may reflect relatively high interest in financial services products, but a preference to consider all the options before committing to a purchase.

Undoubtedly, permission-based e-mail has real potential to become an effective means of communication, provided it can escape the shadow cast by the spammers.

TEXT MESSAGING (SMS)

In many markets, the ownership of mobile phones (cell phones in North America) is very widespread. According to research from GartnerG2, in 2002 62 per cent of all adults in the major European countries used a mobile telephone. In the same year, 41 per cent used SMS, compared to 30 per cent using the Internet, while in the previous year, 28 per cent used SMS compared to 29 per cent using the Internet (*Wise Marketer*, 15 November 2002). Identifying the potential of this new medium, in July 2003 First Direct became the first UK bank to use SMS to promote its services. At the time of writing, results of the test were not available, but in a loyalty programme promotion, TotalFinaElf found that on average 200 customers per filling station signed up for an SMS campaign, and about 10 per cent redeemed the offer after the first of two text messages (*Colloquy*, 16 January 2003). MasterCard has claimed impressive results

Marketing Financial Services through the Internet: Still a Way to Go

Online banks reach at least 30% of the active Internet audience in five key markets. Of all Internet users: in Sweden more than 50%; Australia 40%; France 39%; Netherlands 38%; Brazil 36%, and UK more than 30% visit financial services sites.

Between October 2001 and October 2002, European financial services site visitors increased from 15 million to 25 million, for a total of 37% of all regular visitors (*Nielsen Netratings* January 2003).

- In the UK, 55% of borrowers prefer to deal face to face (*Qualisteam* 27 September 2002, quoting Datamonitor).

- In the UK, 32% of respondents say they have the strongest relationship with a personal bank, compared with only 7% with an Internet bank (*Wise Marketer* 21 February 2003, quoting KPMG).

- In the US, of 60 million customers who sought loan, credit card, insurance or investment information online, 37 million (63%) made their applications off-line (*CardFlash* 12 February 2003, quoting Dieringer).

- In Canada, 19% of banking customers do most of their transactions on the Internet (9% by phone) (*Wise Marketer* 30 January 2003, quoting Maritz Thompson Lightstone).

- In Spain, BankInter's commercial customers conduct 47% of their transactions online (*Desarrollo* 12 June 2002).

- At American Express, 8 million cards have enrolled in the online account service, representing approximately 15% of the company's global card base (*Dow Jones Newswires* 5 December 2002).

Results

1. Retail banks in Europe are re-investing in bricks and mortar, for an annual expenditure estimated at $1 billion by 2005, a compound annual rate of growth of 9.6% from 2002–2005 (*Wise Marketer* 11 November 2002, quoting KPMG).

2. 'The average yield on an interest-paying checking account at a US Internet bank is now 1.84%, a premium of 1.23 percentage points over a traditional bank, according to Bankrate.com. A year ago, Internet banks had an average yield of 3.78%, which was a premium of 2.61 percentage points' (*The Wall Street Journal* April 2002)

3. In the last year, 13 million Europeans, or 11% of the online population, bought finance products online, according to the latest research from Forrester. A wider group of 34% of online consumers in Europe researched a financial product online in that period. Car insurance, shares and current accounts are the most studied products, but users avoid more complicated products like mortgages, life insurance and pensions (*New Media Age* 19 September 2002).

4. Of the £267 billion mortgage lending projected for 2006, £26.7 billion will be sold online, predicts a Datamonitor survey. In the year to June 2002 only 4% of those who bought or arranged a mortgage did so online (*New Media Age* 10 October 2002). In Europe as a whole, Forrester predicts that 5% of mortgages will be originated on the Internet in 2003, with the UK and the Nordic countries leading the way. Remortgagers outnumber first time buyers by three to one in markets like the UK and the Netherlands (*New Media Age* 17 October 2003).

from SMS campaigns in Europe, with response rates approaching 10 per cent in 2002 (*CardFlash*, 13 March 2003).

Clearly, apart from the US where mobile coverage is patchy and text messaging less widely used, there is potential for SMS to convey simple communications.

GETTING CONSENT

Although the rules vary from market to market, and not every jurisdiction is keeping up with the development of new electronic channels of communication, there is a general acceptance of the principle that any organisation delivering a marketing message direct to the consumer must do so with his or her consent. The challenge comes in deciding how that consent should be given. The tougher approach says that a consumer must explicitly agree to receiving communications ('opt in'), while a less rigorous view is that the consumer must explicitly refuse consent ('opt out').

To protect the organisation's reputation, it is crucial for marketers to follow whatever rules have been established, either by law or industry agreement.

DATA CONFIDENTIALITY

Here, the rules vary widely, between the more prescriptive approach of the EU, and the more relaxed standards usual in North America. Once again, marketers must make themselves familiar with their obligations and follow them to the letter.

COMMUNICATIONS CHANNELS COMPARED

Media owners will, understandably enough, place a great deal of emphasis on conventional measures of channel performance such as reach and frequency which, although the names may change, are basic yardsticks for nearly all media. Marketers, however, will see these measures, not as ends in themselves, but simply ways of achieving the business goal, whatever that may be – from soft objectives such as improving brand recognition through to hard ones such as generating sales revenues.

Accordingly, how well the various communication channel options perform will vary from time to time and from organisation to organisation. However, the table in Figure 7.11 provides some useful insights, as it compares actual outcomes on key business measures for different credit card solicitation methods in the US.

On this basis, accounts acquired through the Internet have the worst renewal and activity rates, although the low cost of the medium keeps the break even period down. The lowest break even period appears to come from accounts acquired as a result of a portfolio purchase – an activity in which, it should be noted, the research source operates.

Acquisition channel	Renewal rates (%)	Activity rates (%)	Break even in months
Portfolio acquisition	n/a	n/a	11
Direct mail	80–90	85–90	28
Pre-approved	70–80	80–85	24
Telemarketing	60–70	65–70	36
Pre-approved and telemarketing	55–60	60–65	40
Internet	55–60	50–60	20
Agent bank	65–75	75–85	18
Average	**68**	**82**	**25**

Source: R.K. Hammer Investment Bankers, quoted in *CardFlash* 27 May 2003

Figure 7.11   Comparison of actual outcomes for different credit card solicitation methods in the US

SUMMING UP

To communicate any message successfully, decisions must be taken about:

- what the message is;

- how it is expressed;

- who is the intended audience;

- how we reach them;

- what we want them to do or think or feel as a result of receiving our message.

Many of these decisions will be subjective – Does this really say what I want it to? Are these the best visuals for this market? – and there is no substitute for experience in making them. But many, especially those to do with media choice, will have a much firmer foundation in data.

DISTRIBUTION

In the financial services industry, it may be possible for the communication package also to fulfil the task of distribution.

However, the products being sold are often very complex, and must be tailored carefully to the customer's needs; additionally, the selling process may be covered by regulations which require, for instance, cooling-off periods, written statements of the customer's overall financial situation and anti-money laundering procedures. These will usually make it impossible for the sales process to be completed in one step.

For instance, under Section 326 of the USA Patriot Act, 'banks, insurance companies, credit card companies, money service businesses, mutual funds, broker dealers, and casinos must take steps to verify the identity of account holders and to eliminate financial transactions and flows of money to terrorist organizations' (*CardFlash*, 4 June 2003).

Additionally, if lending products are involved, the customer's credit will have to be checked. In all these cases, the task of communication is usually to generate leads or enquiries which are then handled by a sales person, often in a face-to-face interview (see Figure 7.12).

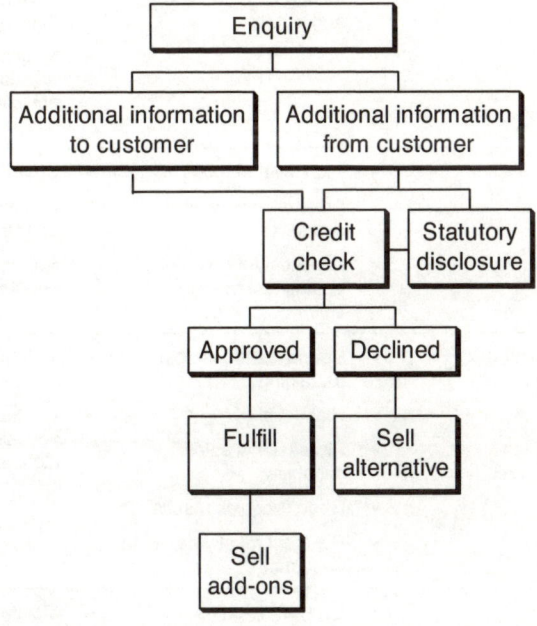

Figure 7.12 Enquiry handling

Whether the sale is handled face to face or on the telephone (less usually on the Internet, except in the case of straightforward lending and insurance products), a sales person has to be employed. The question which then arises is where, from a managerial point of view, the selling function is located. For businesses in the financial services industry, the choices are often between:

- the branch network
- a dedicated internal sales force
- a third party sales force
- intermediaries (for example, brokers and independent financial advisers).

Each of these channels has its strengths and weaknesses as shown in Figure 7.13. Some suggested strategies for dealing with the weaknesses are also shown in Figure 7.14.

Channel	Strengths	Weaknesses
Branch network	• Low or no incremental costs • Known in-house standards of training and quality	• May be responsible for selling hundreds of products • Sales may in practice have a lower priority than service • Motivating and rewarding sales achievement may be difficult
Dedicated internal sales force	• High level of focus • Professional sales capability • Essential for complex or long, drawn-out sales	• Protracted set-up times • Expensive to recruit and reward • May fit badly in service-oriented organisation
Third party sales force	• Set-up costs restricted to training • High level of focus • Professional sales capability • Good for quick results • Payment mostly based on results	• Maintaining standards can be tricky • Contra-indicated for upscale products or high value clients
Intermediaries	• Low set-up costs • Payment by results only	• Maintaining standards can be tricky • Contra-indicated for upscale products or high value clients

Figure 7.13   Strengths and weaknesses of different selling channels

BRANCH NETWORKS

Recent research is re-emphasising the importance of the branch's role as 'the most important channel for delivery, service, sales, reinforcing the bank's brand, strengthening customer relationships, and selling non-traditional, consultative products such as investments and wealth management' (*Wise Marketer*, 26 June 2003, quoting *Financial Insights*). Often, however, branch networks are controlled by a

Channel	Weaknesses	Strategies
Branch network	• May be responsible for selling hundreds of products • Sales may in practice have a lower priority than service • Encouraging and rewarding sales achievement may be difficult	• Appoint dedicated Branch Liaison Manager • Nominate best-performing branches as 'Pacesetters' and export their techniques to other branches • Identify product champion in each branch • Set up performance leagues with appropriate rewards
Dedicated internal sales force	• Protracted set-up times • Expensive to recruit and reward • May fit badly in service-oriented organisation	• Start early • Recruit internally, where possible • Position membership of sales force as aspirational for other staff
Third party sales force and intermediaries	• Maintaining standards can be tricky • Contra-indicated for upscale products or high value clients	• Appoint dedicated manager • Train carefully • Use mystery shoppers to observe standards • Incentivise quality as well as sales • Use only where appropriate

Figure 7.14 Suggested strategies for dealing with weaknesses

powerful manager with considerable seniority and influence within the organisation, whose agenda may well be far different from yours. Persuading such an individual to pay attention to your product is often one of the biggest challenges a marketer has to face.

Effectively, what we are trying to do is sell the product, of course, but to a specialised and very small audience. A good place to start, therefore, is to consider from the manager's point of view the question 'What's in it for me?' Despite his godlike status, the network manager is usually just as keen on pleasing his boss as lesser mortals, and this is where once again we see the power of getting support at the most senior possible level. We can now answer the 'What's in it for me?' question by saying, as diplomatically as necessary, 'The CEO has indicated that this is a product he personally supports; there are sound business reasons for his opinion, which are…' Getting access to the network manager can be another challenge, which may be resolved by asking one's own boss to set up the meeting.

As with any other negotiation, it is crucial to know what range of outcomes we would accept. Perhaps the best result of all would be to have targets for our product built into the annual performance goals of branch and district managers; as a minimum, we might accept getting approved access to the branches for training and motivation purposes. Between these two extremes, the table in Figure 7.14 gives some examples of techniques which have been proven to work.

DEDICATED INTERNAL SALES FORCE

Financial services organisations stand at both extremes of the spectrum of ability to manage sales forces. At one end, retail banks as a whole have only an indifferent record: the essentially outward-looking, results-driven, iconoclastic culture of a successful sales force often sits uneasily with the more process-driven thinking of large banking organisations. Additionally, the high rewards demanded and earned by top-ranking sales people can generate jealous criticism from other staff.

At the other extreme, some insurers and stock-brokers have so strongly emphasised the selling function that they have been criticised for the aggressive tactics adopted by their bonus-hungry sales people.

There are techniques for dealing with both these sets of issues. In the case of the organisation which has not historically had a strong direct sales component:

- Ensure that the whole organisation understands the crucial role of the sales force: that by creating new business, they create new employment opportunities for everyone.

- Take every opportunity to involve staff from other departments in the sales process – and ensure that their contribution is widely known and recognised.

- Position the sales force as an effective and highly rated group, access to which is open to anyone with the right skills and ambitions.

- Emphasise consistently that the most successful sales people are those who listen to customers, not those who talk at them.

Organisations which have been overly aggressive in their sales policies might wish to:

- Stress that the most profitable relationships are those with satisfied customers, who are willing to buy more, and recommend your business to their friends.

- Ensure that the sales force remuneration package includes a modest basic salary so that sales people are not completely reliant on quick – and possibly inappropriate – sales to generate income.

- Emphasise that selling against the customer's best interests is a career-threatening activity.

All this, of course, should be in addition to ensuring that, where necessary, sales people have the appropriate professional qualifications, and thoroughly understand and follow the regulatory requirements for the products they sell. It should go without saying that product training (induction, refreshers and updates) is absolutely essential for anyone carrying out a sales function, no matter where they are formally located within the organisation.

THIRD PARTY SALES FORCE

Circumstances can arise when it makes sense to work with a third party sales force. Instances could involve a short-term requirement for additional resource such as at programme launch, or mounting a large-scale promotion: a typical example would be the sales people used to acquire new insurance or credit card customers at airports or in shopping malls. Occasionally, there may be a need for specialist skills or contacts, such as selling financial services to a particular type of industry.

Essentially, the challenges centre around quality control: how to ensure that the sales person targets the right kind of prospect with the right product and sells it in the right way. There is no substitute for training and monitoring: training to ensure that the appropriate standards are communicated, monitoring to ensure that they are implemented. 'Mystery shoppers' are an effective way of checking performance. Where sales people earn commissions, records should be rigorously audited, not just at acquisition, but over time, to ensure that new accounts are correctly managed in all respects. It is rarely wise to adopt a hands-off approach: scrutiny should be constant and visible.

Properly handled, the third party sales force can be a valuable addition to the in-house capability. If resources are insufficient for a high level of supervision, it would be best to find an alternative.

INTERMEDIARIES

In some segments of the financial services market, intermediaries – who may be called agents or brokers – have historically played an important role in distribution. Traditionally in the UK, much life and property insurance business has been placed through brokers, and borrowers now often source home loans through intermediaries.

For principals, the strength of the agency as a route to market is that, as an independent organisation, it is motivated to go out and find business on its own account. But this brings a corresponding weakness: the agency sees the client as its own, not the principal's. And the same may be true in reverse – clients see themselves as having a relationship with the agency, not the principal. Consequently, there is an additional challenge in ensuring share of sales as, in the interest of their clients and their own commercial freedom, few brokers will tie themselves exclusively to one provider. Finally, as with the third party sales force, quality control is a constant issue. Although many intermediary channels are overseen by a professional body (for example, the British Insurance Brokers' Association) which sets standards for various aspects of conduct and business management, prudence still dictates careful supervision.

Taken together, these considerations will almost certainly call for setting up a sales function to manage the intermediary channel. This can still be more cost-effective than going direct, but the balance between the two options is sometimes a fine one.

Accordingly, perhaps the biggest threat to agents and brokers is 'disintermediation', where providers see an opportunity to cut costs and re-assert control over product distribution by selling direct to the public, often through a website.

Whatever the communication and distribution channel chosen for the product, it is vital to plan the numbers involved. The example in Figure 7.15 is based on a direct sales force selling life insurance, but the same principles would apply to any channel or product.

The expense and visibility of creating a dedicated sales force are matched only by the potential returns – and the risk if it fails to deliver.

	Per annum £
Base salary	20 000
Other employment expense	5 000
Bonus	10 000
Total compensation	35 000
Car and subsistence cost	8 000
Total	**£43 000**

Days in year	365
Holidays	20
Weekends and public holidays	120
Illness	2
Total non-working days	142
Working days	223
Days at office*	48
Training	10
Total non-selling days	58
Selling days	165
Average calls per day	2.5
Total calls	413
Cost per call	£104
Average sales rate**	40%
Average cost per successful call	**£261**

* 1 per working week
** Qualified leads

	Per annum
Sales budget	£150 000 000
Average value per sale	£100 000
Target number of policies	1 500
Average completed sales per sales person	165
Number of salespeople needed	9
Total cost of sales force	**£387 000**

*Ignores cost of lead generation, occupancy and
communications, support staff and management time.*

Figure 7.15   The cost of a salesman

COMPARING COMMUNICATION AND DISTRIBUTION CHANNELS

Almost certainly, some combination of channels will work more effectively than focussing on just one way of getting the product to market. But balancing the competing claims of *reach* (how big an audience is exposed to the message or product), *frequency* (how often), *targeting* (how many of the audience are people we want to reach), *impact* (how the message cuts through other messages) and *cost* is always a major exercise, and often contentious. Which combination is best for a particular case is a matter of judgement, supported by analysis of whatever data is available. As a benchmark, the table in Figure 7.16 provides an indication of the performance of some of the major channels in the US credit card industry.

	Per account	Response
Portfolio acquisition	$40–$230	n/a
Direct mail	$95–$115	0.3%–0.7%
Pre-approved	$70–$90	0.6%–1.8%
Telemarketing	$60–$70	3.0%–6.0%
Pre-approved and telemarketing	$50–$60	4.0%–5.0%
Internet application	$10–$45	0.6%–2.1%
Agent banks	$10–$40	1.2%–2.6%
Average	$78	

Costs include marketing, bureau expense, credit processing and card issuance
Source: R.K. Hammer Investment Bankers, quoted in *CardFlash* 9 April 2003

Figure 7.16   Credit card account acquisition costs

SUMMING UP

How financial services products are distributed can mean success or failure: for example, the success of travellers cheque issuers depends almost completely on the ability of their sales forces to make an (effectively) exclusive sales contract with major distributors such as banks, travel agencies and motoring associations. But, while for some products there is little choice about what channel to use, for others the possibilities are much wider. In these cases, it is sensible to make regular tests of the efficiency of the different options.

CHAPTER 8

Getting Management Approval

INTRODUCTION

In many organisations, there is a highly developed process for securing management approval for investment projects. Often, this will involve making applications through a process of submitting the proposal in a particular format, meeting specific criteria, and making a presentation to a committee which meets regularly to consider marketing investment projects. Shorn of its superstructure, however, this is a situation which basically calls for selling skills; the chances of success will improve significantly if we adopt the salesman's approach: 'What do they want? How does my product meet what they are looking for? How can I demonstrate this best?'

THE APPROVAL PROCESS

In financial service institutions particularly, with their long experience in making decisions on applications for credit or investment, there is likely to be a very formal approach to approving substantial marketing projects – taking 'substantial' to mean long term and/or high visibility as well as the more usual implication of high cost. Most of the time, the fundamental issue for the decision-makers is an economic one: how to allocate scarce resources among many competing claims.

However, it is quite likely that overlaid on this question will be a variety of supplementaries relating to what the organisation currently sees as its strategic focus – and it is not meant to be dismissive of senior management to say that this focus can and does change over time, according to real or perceived imperatives. For example, a bank's CEO may have set the business a target of cutting distribution costs: under these circumstances, an investment project will be more likely to get a go-ahead if it uses the Internet rather than bricks-and-mortar to get to market. To ensure that these goals are recognised and implemented throughout the bank, they may well be built into the personal objectives of the manager or managers who make the investment decision – and how well they achieve those objectives will determine their bonus and promotion prospects. From the beginning of the concept, it would be wise to take into account any biases of this sort.

It is a truism that one of the most frequent tasks facing management is making decisions with incomplete data. Nowhere is this more common than investing in new products or services: the funds required are usually large (and the cynic's foreboding is usually correct: what is asked for is rarely as much as what is actually spent) and the return on the investment by no means sure. To make the decision still more difficult, there are likely to be far more projects than there are resources to fund and service them all.

Some means has to be found to identify the projects which the organisation is prepared to back.

A few organisations go entirely on gut feel – but they are in a very small minority, and are likely to be run by highly entrepreneurial individuals who either own the business or have a very great deal of authority in it. Even then, it makes sense for the marketer to get to know what is currently on the boss's mind, and make a case accordingly. The strength of such a system is that it very often generates fast decisions, and projects which are approved usually have the imprimatur of endorsement by the boss stamped very clearly on them. The major weakness of the approach is that, because all decisions are made by one individual, and that individual is human with changing priorities and concerns, it will not be consistent or transparent. Another challenge with this management structure is actually getting into the boss's diary.

Far more likely, especially in financial service institutions, is a self-consciously systematic approach, with clear objectives to be met, and a highly detailed process for making the proposal, even down to a battery of forms to be completed. At the heart of these procedures is usually the requirement to meet financial objectives: these have already been discussed in Chapter 6, and in a well-thought-out project should pose no problem. Surrounding this relatively hard centre, however, are likely to be layers of successively softer criteria – softer in the sense that the extent to which the project meets them is more a matter of opinion and presentation than the relatively objective requirements of pounds and pennies.

These additional criteria will probably include standard marketing measures – share of wallet, market share and so on – which have also been dealt with in Chapter 6. But there could well be additional standards to be met which reflect current management strategic thinking or business priorities or statutory requirements. Examples might include the following.

Management strategic thinking

- exploitation of organisation-wide synergies
- using the branch network more intensively
- becoming a financial supermarket
- building share in consumer lending.

Business priorities

- 're-engineering' to cut costs
- improving cross-sell performance

- reducing attrition.

Statutory requirements

- avoidance of discriminatory behaviour
- honesty in lending
- compliance with legal standards set for the sales process.

So as to paint the most favourable picture possible, all of these potential criteria need to be borne carefully in mind from the planning stage onwards, to ensure that no potentially embarrassing corners are cut – or potentially powerful points not made.

The other dimension which it is vital to consider is the risk inherent in the project. Although by most standards £1 million is a good deal of money, many large organisations would see it as only a modest investment. For others, however, losing £1 million may spell ruin.

Equally, risk has dimensions other than the purely monetary: a financial services institution relies heavily on its reputation for probity and fair dealing, and anything which could potentially put that in jeopardy would be unlikely to get approval. Nor would a large organisation with many business partnerships willingly wish to endanger those relationships, unless the potential return were very high. I once suggested to a business that it would be much cheaper for them to buy their own training centre rather than continue to spend very large sums of money each year to hire meeting rooms in hotels. The recommendation was turned down flat: although at one level the argument was sound, the overall value of the commercial relationship which the business had with the hotel chains involved was far in excess of any savings to be had from annoying them by taking the facility in-house.

However, all these criteria are by definition general: they will be applied to every investment project the business might consider, from upgrading its ATMs to launching a new investment trust. It often makes sense to establish criteria particular to the project in hand.

In the case of the Netherlands loyalty programme launch mentioned on page 5, for example, the Management Committee established requirements which had to be met by successive phases of the business roll-out.

For instance, in phase 2 of the feasibility study, the project team had to provide answers to these questions:

- How big would the market be?
- Would the scheme be legal?
- How would members be enrolled?
- What would be the tax implications for savers and issuers of points?

- How would points be awarded and credited to savers' accounts?

- Would it be possible to set up a call centre to answer requests for information and award redemptions?

- What would be the systems requirements?

- How would the scheme be structured so as to be attractive to collectors while affordably creating the changes in buying preferences sought by the partners?

A further example comes from North America, where a large bank was considering setting up a regional marketing programme. This was to be a so-called 'coalition' scheme, in that the bank would work with partners from selected industries. Early on in the thinking, senior management established a basic requirement that the partner grouping should include a supermarket, a petrol distributor and at least one other retail chain. Further criteria also covered such issues as partners' market share, systems capability and so on.

This also illustrates another important principle: making it easy for senior management to say Yes. Where a major investment is at issue, it can make sense to break the project into separate steps, each one of which calls for increasing levels of expenditure, but by meeting its own set of criteria, lays a firm basis for the next step in the process. This approach provides the comfort that increasing commitment is matched by increasing evidence that the project is likely to succeed.

BUILDING THE BUSINESS CASE

Although a full-scale phased approach may not be applicable to smaller marketing projects, nevertheless it includes several important principles in getting management approval:

- making it easy to say Yes (or conversely, minimising the number of reasons for saying No)

- drawing together a number of separate strands to present a comprehensive, coherent and integrated plan

- a prudent approach to risk management

- demonstrating one's mastery of the material.

These principles apply to developing business cases for the smallest as well as the very largest management undertakings.

The five phases may be summarised as follows:

Phase 1: preliminary survey

Outline responses, probably based on desk research, to the questions set out in previous chapters:

- product definition
- market definition
- customer definition
- financial and marketing measures
- communication and distribution.

Phase 2: feasibility study

- confirming the assumptions of the preliminary survey, probably by specially commissioned market research
- refining and presenting the data in much more detail
- SWOT analysis
- gap analysis
- formulating viability criteria/key points for success/risk assessment.

Phase 3: developing a business plan

Producing an integrated set of plans to cover:

- business goals and objectives
- marketing
- distribution channel management
- operations
- IT/systems
- human resources
- financials
- legal and other approvals
- risk assessment
- exit strategy.

Phase 4: launch

- Execution of the agreed plans.

Phase 5: post-launch management

- Monitoring performance against planned goals.
- Taking remedial action where necessary.
- Incorporating new targets as the business develops.

Each of these phases is discussed in detail in the next chapters.

To Launch or Not to Launch?

A banking group was considering launching a Fleet Card. Aimed at businesses operating large numbers of vehicles, this is a product allowing drivers to buy fuel, pay for on-the-road repairs, and other defined expenses; it also has extensive control and reporting features. The issues identified for the first phase were:

Phase 1

Product definition
- What features should the product have?
- What do competing products do?
- What are customers looking for – tomorrow, as well as today?

Technical
- What technical infrastructure is needed to support it
  – at petrol stations?
  – at the transaction processing centre?
  – at the customer servicing centre?
- How much of this already exists?
- Where there are gaps, how much would it cost to fill them, and how long would it take?

Marketing
- Who are the key competitors, and what are their strengths and weaknesses?
- How should the product be distributed?

Profitability
- Would the product be profitable in its own right?
- What is the market size?
- How much of it is already penetrated by competing products?
- What are the estimates for revenues and costs?

In fact, the last marketing question became the key test for Phase 2 of the project. While the bank's own branches might be expected to sell at least some Fleet Cards, the most important distribution channel in this particular market was likely to be vehicle leasing companies, the biggest of which belonged to another bank, which was unlikely to want to sell a competitor's product.

Once satisfactory answers had been generated to the Phase 1 questions, the issue therefore became would the bank's own leasing company be prepared to add the Fleet Card to its own product range?

The Fleet Card example illustrates the point that the final decision on a project may be taken outside the organisation which is developing it. Under these circumstances, it makes sense to discover what priorities the third party has. In this particular case, a review of the vehicle leasing market indicated that it was highly competitive, and that there was great pressure on prices. Discreet internal enquiries suggested that the bank's own leasing business was suffering from the same profitability squeeze as the rest of the industry. Accordingly, the project sponsors decided to approach the leasing company on the basis that the card was an easy sell which would immediately boost the leasing company's revenues.

Under other circumstances it would be appropriate to choose some other positioning. For example, if the leasing company had been feeling no pricing pressure, it may have been more persuasive to adopt the approach that this was a highly technically advanced product which would significantly strengthen the leasing company's product range.

Again, what is appropriate for organisations is equally appropriate to individuals: whether the decision will be made by one person or a committee, it is always sensible to find out what are their prejudices, and ensure that the proposal reflects them. For instance, where an investment committee is made up of representatives from different parts of the organisation, they will very often have two sets of criteria in mind: 'How will this affect the business unit which I represent?', and 'How does this meet my own particular set of business beliefs?' Time spent on identifying a decision-maker's hot buttons is time well spent. It may even be a sound idea to develop a formal strategy to deal with the known perspectives of each of the managers involved.

Academics and practitioners have made many attempts to describe how managers arrive at decisions; there is a kernel of truth in most of them, and the model which follows is as good as any. Essentially, it identifies five types of decision-maker:

> *Charismatics* can be initially exuberant about a new idea or proposal, but will yield a decision based on a balanced set of information.

> *Thinkers* can exhibit contrary points of view in a single meeting and need to cautiously work through all the options before coming to a decision.

> *Sceptics* remain highly suspicious of data that don't fit their worldview and make decisions based on their gut feelings.

> *Followers* make decisions based on how other trusted executives, or they themselves, have made similar decisions in the past.

> *Controllers* focus on the pure facts and analytics of a decision because of their own fears and uncertainties.

> (Williams and Miller, *Harvard Business Review*, May 2002)

Intuitively, this typology, which is based on extensive research, feels broadly right. Where a single executive is making the decision, it would make sense to make as good an assessment as possible of his or her style – colleagues may be willing to share their experiences – and tailor the whole presentation to suit. More difficult is the common case where a committee is responsible for reviewing the proposal: even so, it would be possible to develop an approach designed to appeal to its most powerful member, but also having available materials and arguments which will respond to the other executives' temperaments

Another useful technique for securing management approval is the 'white knight' strategy. This involves getting one of the decision-makers or influencers (see below) to become the project's champion. Usually, this means that the project happens to chime with a particular enthusiasm or priority which the individual is known to have. The decision-maker not only then lends his or her own authority to the project, but can be relied on to push for it in the informal exchanges away from the committee context which can often be very important in building a consensus for approval.

These informal exchanges often include people who are outside the official group of decision-makers but nevertheless have opinions which carry weight with those ultimately responsible for taking the formal decision. What makes their opinion matter can vary: sometimes they are elder statesmen, whose endorsement carries weight because of their long experience with the company. Others may be technical experts, or users, or rising management stars, who do not actually sit on the committee, but whose views on the project's practicality will be asked for. These influencers can clearly be important in shaping the final outcome, and it is worth establishing who they are, and working out how to get their approval with just as much care as one would for the decision-makers themselves.

Very often, it is valuable to pull all these threads together, and develop a detailed campaign for selling the project.

In the situation outlined in Figure 8.1, for example, the decision-makers and influencers all have widely-different objectives and hot buttons. Luckily, none are in direct conflict – though this would be not at all unusual – and it should be possible to craft a case for the project which meets all the requirements. Where pivotal deciders have clashing priorities, the only solution often is to decide which of them carries most weight and play to him or her, without of course alienating the other executive, who could well have power to delay or even block the project.

In terms of how the pitch should be made, a great deal will depend on what is the norm for the company, and what are the preferences of the executives involved. For instance, some managers would rather see the broad outlines of the business case presented in a PowerPoint presentation, with the details in a separate written handout; others feel more comfortable going through all the material step by step. In any case, it is usually a good idea to present a summary of the argument at the very beginning of the presentation, to minimise the risk of getting stuck on the detail before getting to the main point; it also ensures that, if any of the decision-makers has

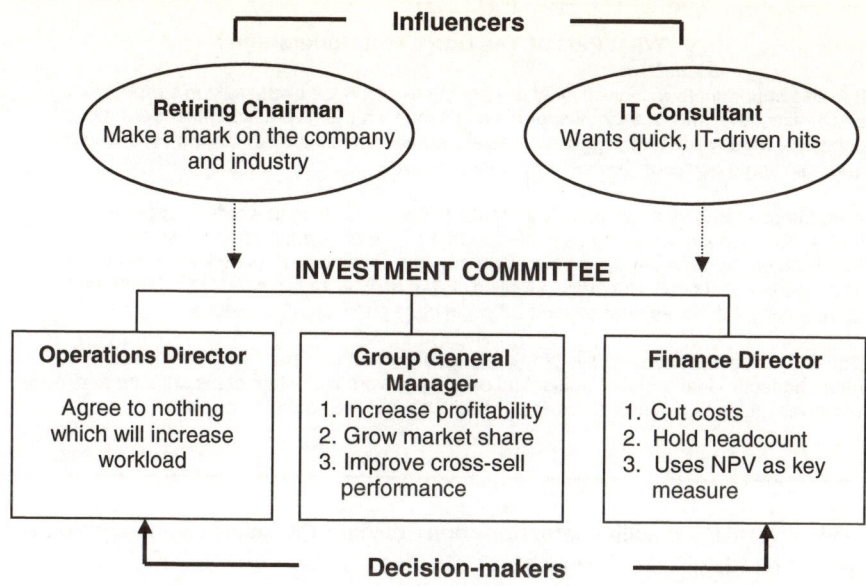

Figure 8.1   Varied goals in decision-making

to leave early (discourteous, but not unknown), at least they have heard the main outline of the case, and any questions they have can be dealt with before they go.

One of the biggest challenges is deciding whether or not to circulate the papers ahead of time. If they have to be distributed before the meeting, it is absolutely essential that they tell the whole story: a skilled and persuasive presenter can use an outline PowerPoint presentation simply as a set of prompts for an oral presentation, providing the detail and expanding the points as they go through the slides. But the ability to sweep an audience along by enthusiasm and rhetoric simply doesn't work where a decision-maker is reading the file, perhaps on a train or plane. Nor is this technique recommended where many facts and figures have to be presented.

Overall, it is usually best to include all relevant material into the presentation, spelling out the argument by using a carefully considered structure, and reinforcing it by frequent reminders and summaries. With this in mind, before the document is circulated, it is usually a good idea to get the reactions to it from people who are unconnected with the project: closeness to a topic can often lead to errors of logic, presentation and content which are obvious to others, but not so clear to the person who has created the document. Tangible supports often make a difference: draft layouts of ads or mailing packs can add a spark of excitement and bring an abstract concept powerfully to life. Even here, though, it is prudent to respect individual preferences: it is probably unwise to show a lavishly produced, fully edited TV commercial to a group of known penny-pinchers. Above all else, do not read the slides out: nothing is more calculated to lose the attention of the audience, who can read the words much faster than you can say them.

What Part of Yes Don't You Understand?

It is also important to recognise what is a buying signal: once I was making a proposal to a senior executive who was famous for his reluctance ever to give a straight answer. On this occasion, what was being suggested was somewhat outside the company's usual thinking, and from some points of view set a precedent – always a worry for some managers.

After the pitch was over, my boss launched into his usual cloud of words. I had invited along for the occasion a newly-hired executive so that he could be introduced to senior management and see the decision-making process at first hand. As we left, he said to me, 'Well, we lost that one.' 'Not at all,' I replied. 'What he was saying was "Do it, but don't embarrass me if it goes pear-shaped".' I could have been wrong, of course…

Equally, I once saw an executive plough doggedly on with his pitch long after it had been made perfectly clear that the project had been approved: the failure of his antenna to pick up what was happening risked his selling himself into and then out of approval.

Finally, this is a selling situation: don't disdain the salesperson's techniques – listen out for buying signals, look for closure.

SUMMING UP

The process of getting management approval for the project is essentially one of selling the idea: the mere fact that the 'customer' is an internal audience rather than an outside client should make no difference to the way in which we approach it. Just as if one were selling any other kind of product, it will always pay to:

- ensure that all the organisation's formal criteria are satisfied;

- make the decision easy, if necessary by splitting it up into pieces of acceptable size;

- understand the personal goals and prejudices of the decision-makers;

- discover who else is likely to influence the decision, and get their buy-in;

- rehearse the presentation to ensure mastery of the material, and uncover any weaknesses in time to fix them;

- use visual supports and back-up to add excitement and reality to the project.

CHAPTER 9

From Feasibility Study to Business Plan

INTRODUCTION

How a project moves from getting initial management sign-off to full budgetary approval will vary with the programme's size, and any procedures the organisation has set up to handle this process. Most commonly, management will ask the product champion to verify the assumptions made in the first proposals. This stage of verifying the assumptions is often called a feasibility study or viability study, but the name used is much less important than the process. If the outcomes are positive – and they may well be somewhat different from what had originally been envisaged – the next step is to use the findings as the basis for developing a full business plan. This will be the document submitted to senior management for their final approval and the corresponding authority to commit resources.

Essentially at this stage we are aiming to provide answers to the questions 'Will this work? If so, what do we need to do to make it happen?'

MOVING BEYOND THE EDUCATED GUESS

Where those assumptions were made on the basis of desk research, they will now need to be reinforced by specific research studies. If broad estimates of costs and revenues were used, these will need to be refined, by getting quotations from suppliers. Timings will need to be reviewed, especially where operations or customer service are involved, or where staff need to be recruited: all of these things take longer than you would like or expect. Particular care needs to be taken where processes are already outsourced to third parties: any changes to agreed responsibilities and functions will need to be carefully negotiated, bearing in mind that many outsourcing organisations expect to generate their profits by driving a very hard bargain at this stage, knowing that they have a strong negotiating position.

This is also the point at which internal plans have to be shared with outsiders: confidentiality must be protected. If the outside organisations do not already have a non-disclosure or confidentiality agreement, it is essential that they execute one before any material is shared with them, or discussions take place. If an agreement already exists, make sure that it is still valid: many agreements have expiry dates and it has been known for a supplier not to remind a customer of the fact, hoping to put the information learned to his own advantage. More positively, suppliers' experience can often lead to savings of time and money, or avoid expensive mistakes being made.

A practical way of ensuring the effectiveness of this stage of the planning process is to compile a list of questions which the feasibility study has to answer as shown in Figure 9.1.

Area	Possible criteria
Marketing	What is the customer proposition?
	How will the product be branded?
	What does research predict will be the target market's reaction?
	How will the product be distributed?
	What will the marketing launch plan be?
	What budgets should be set for sales revenues and marketing costs?
Customer service/ Operations	How will the product be serviced?
	What resources will be needed?
IT/Systems	What IT support will the product need before, during and after sales?
	How long will it take to develop and test any new functionality?
	What will it cost to provide?
	Who will provide it?
Human resources	Would additional posts need to be created?
	How would they be documented, compensated and filled?
	What would be the training requirement?
	Is this achievable within the programme time scale?
Financials	What investment will be required? When and how?
	Will the investment meet internal targets?
	Are the budgeting, reporting and control processes adequate?
Legal and other approvals	Does the programme meet all internal and external legal and procedural requirements?
Risk assessment	What risks does the programme pose for the organisation?
	How serious are they?
	What would be our response to them if they were to be realised?
Exit strategy	If the programme needs to be terminated, how would we do this?
	What steps would we need to take with regard to customers, commercial partners, staff, and the general public?

Figure 9.1 Setting decision criteria

DEVELOPING THE BUSINESS PLAN

Above all, this is a time for drawing together all the threads which will be involved in launching the project. Each element will require the development of a separate plan; together, these blueprints will form the business plan for the entire programme.

Depending on the nature of the project, the elements to be covered are likely to include:

- business goals and objectives
- marketing
- distribution channel management
- operations
- IT/systems
- human resources
- financials
- legal and other approvals
- risk assessment
- exit strategy.

The format of the plan may be determined by company policy. If not, the general outline of one possible approach follows; it has been developed on the basis that Acme Bank is looking to improve the performance of one of its key divisions.

The value of this particular approach to developing a business plan is the discipline it imposes on its compilers to document:

- The key objectives to be achieved by each business group;
- The tasks necessary to accomplish these objectives, together with
  - their cost
  - the results expected
  - the date by which the task is to be accomplished
  - who is responsible for them.

Accordingly, it provides a useful checklist against which progress can subsequently be reviewed.

ACME FINANCIAL SERVICES

NEWSCHEME

DRAFT OUTLINE BUSINESS PLAN

PHASE II:

FROM APPROVAL IN PRINCIPLE TO PROGRAMME LAUNCH

Date

Prepared by

BUSINESS GOALS AND OBJECTIVES

BACKGROUND

Acme Bank is the number three credit card issuer in the national market, as measured by accounts open, and balances revolved:

Issuer	Accounts open	Balances revolved
Universal	7.0 million	$15 billion
Galactic	6.0 million	$10 billion
Acme	4.5 million	$9 billion
Planetary	3.0 million	$4.5 billion
National	2.5 million	$6.5 billion

Source: Knowledge Inc.

The Five Year Plan 'Building on Success' approved by the Bank Board has set the goal of becoming the number two issuer within three years. Additionally, meeting the plan's financial targets for the Division will call for a substantial improvement on all key performance measures.

OBJECTIVES

Accordingly, the Division has agreed these outline business targets:

	Year 1	Year 2	Year 3
Accounts open (million)	5.5	6.0	6.5
Balances revolved ($ billion)	11	12.5	14
Activation rate	75%	80%	85%
Average spend per account	$2000	$2500	$2800
Attrition rate	13%	11%	10%

Source: 'Building on Success' p32

PROGRAMMES

A number of specific action steps are being planned in support of these objectives. This document deals with Newscheme, a proposed coalition loyalty programme which is expected to be the central marketing initiative during the planning period.

RATIONALE

After modelling all the options available to meet the objectives set by the

Division, a coalition loyalty programme has been selected because overall, loyalty is projected to perform better on key portfolio metrics than the other options studied. Appendix 1 gives details of the options reviewed, models used and assumptions made.

A coalition programme has been preferred because it:

- provides a stronger motivation to bank customers to participate in the programme by offering the widest possible opportunity to collect points;

- spreads fixed costs (marketing, customer service, systems and start-up expense) over more sponsors. This
  - reduces the bank's commitment,
  - increases the proportion of the budget available for rewards, thereby increasing the programme's consumer attractiveness;

- increases programme visibility;

- spreads reserve fund liability over all the sponsors;

- allows the bank to strengthen its relationships with key corporate customers.

MARKETING

Objective: Create marketing platform necessary to develop and launch Newscheme programme

KEY TASKS	PROGRAMMES	RESPONSIBILITY	DATE	COST	TARGET
1. Finalise customer proposition	–Validate by consumer market research –Decide launch offer –With Finance, evaluate financials		L minus 90	Research $100,000	Create proposition which balances consumer attractiveness with cost-effectiveness
2. Confirm brand name	–Validate by consumer market research		L minus 90	4 focus groups est. $60,000	Develop distinctive identity
3. Finalise launch arrangements	a. *Create Welcome Pack* –Agree contents (for each partner) –Design cards –Identify card manufacturer/pack assembler –Agree consumer data requirement –Agree collector sign-on incentive –Finalise text and design of carrier, letter, leaflet and outer envelope –Agree distribution methods –Identify data entry services provider		In stock L minus 90	Target cost including mailing $2.25 per pack	Create recruitment pack which is attractive, effective in generating data, simple to complete and process, and cost-effective Total of 1.2 million packs

Finalise launch arrangements continued				
b. Arrange in-store/in-branch launch (ACME and partners) –Agree staff incentive –Train staff –Identify promo. sales force provider –Train promo. staff –Design POS –Manufacturer and distribute POS		Completed L minus 5	–Incentive budget TBC –Promo. sales force est. $200 000 –Training (incl. T&E) $50 000 –POS materials $100,000	Generate 200 000 enrolments, including TBC approved card apps at fully loaded acquisition cost of $65 per approved account
c. Create and mail acquisition/migration DM campaign –Identify and brief agency –Agree creative and targeting proposals –Execute		Available L minus 5	TBC once approval target agreed	Generate 800 000 enrolments, including TBC approved card apps at fully loaded acquisition cost of $85 per approved account
d. Create and build website –Agree content and links to loyalty platform/call centre/redemption and fulfilment house –Identify and brief provider(s) –Approve proposals –Execute		Tested and ready L minus 5	TBC once approval target agreed	Generate 50 000 enrolments, including TBC approved card apps at fully loaded acquisition cost of $25 per approved account

Finalise launch arrangements continued	*e. Create and run media advertising* –Identify and brief agency –Agree creative and media proposals –Buy media –Execute		Executions and schedule approved L minus 10	TBC once approval target agreed	Generate 100 000 enrolments, including TBC approved card apps at target acquisition cost of $150 per approved account
	f. Create and run PR campaign –Identify and brief agency –Agree creative and media proposals –Execute		Creative and media proposals approved L minus 5	Budget $50 000	Support other launch activity
	g. Make arrangements to handle incoming Newscheme card enrolments – all channels –With call centre/ operations, agree traffic volumes for account set-up –Agree and implement staff training programme		Staff trained and systems tested L minus 10	–Training in-house –Systems modifications $80 000	Ensure efficient processing of Newscheme card applications

| **Finalise launch** arrangements continued | *h. Make arrangements to handle incoming credit card apps – all channels* –With Risk Management, agree approval criteria –With Operations, agree traffic volumes for decisioning and account set-up | | Staff trained and systems tested L minus 10 | –Training in-house –Systems modifications $80 000 | Ensure efficient processing of credit card applications |

BUSINESS DEVELOPMENT

Objective: Identify, recruit and negotiate with selected merchants in order to support basic elements of Newscheme concept

KEY TASKS	PROGRAMMES	RESPONSIBILITY	DATE	COST	TARGET
Finalise merchant proposition	Work with identified core partners to agree their business model				Develop offer from range of merchants which maximises collection opportunities, visibility, consumer attainability and appeal, while offering satisfactory ROI to the merchant
Decide NewCo/BankBusiness option	Work with partners and Acme financial and legal advisors to identify most effective business structure				Meet agreed financial, legal and marketing criteria for business structure
Secondary partners	–Identify target list –Negotiate entry –Include in marketing proposition				–Enhance collection opportunities and visibility of programme –Generate additional revenues: $X fees, $Y incremental points revenues, $Z marketing support

FINANCE

Objective: Ensure business models are financially sound and meet Acme criteria; provide support to Business Development in creating partner models; establish budgeting and management reporting capability

KEY TASKS	PROGRAMMES	RESPONSIBILITY	DATE & COST	TARGET
Finalise models	Develop Acme models			–Validate Newscheme's effectiveness as card acquisition, usage enhancement and retention programme –Validate financial soundness of Newscheme as stand-alone business
	Evaluate NewCo/ BankBusiness options			Ensure chosen option is most effective structure from financial and tax standpoint
	Develop individual partner models			Support Business Devopment in creating flexible, effective modelling structures
Advise on management of Reserve Fund	Consult taxation and legal authorities			Ensure Fund provides properly for collector redemptions while allowing surplus funds to be taken to profit
Review sales and income tax implications	Consult taxation and legal authorities			Ensure all tax obligations are properly provided for
Establish systems for budgeting and management reporting				Ensure financial and portfolio performance targets are met

CUSTOMER SERVICE/OPERATIONS

Objective: Create ability to meet Newscheme customer service requirements

KEY TASKS	PROGRAMMES	RESPONSIBILITY	DATE & COST	TARGET
Decide between in-house and outsourcing options	Evaluate cost/service trade-offs			Ensure optimal service provided at competitive cost
Build links to website and incoming customer numbers				Provide comprehensive, effective communications and servicing infrastructure
Build links to loyalty platform and rewards providers				Provide comprehensive, effective communications and servicing infrastructure
Recruit and train staff			Completed L minus 5	Ensure proper provision of trained and motivated staff
Process incoming Newscheme card enrolments –all channels			Built and tested L minus 5	Ensure efficient treatment of incoming enrolments: targets by channel to be confirmed
Process incoming credit card applications – all channels			Built and tested L minus 5	Ensure efficient treatment of incoming applications: targets by channel to be confirmed

CUSTOMER SERVICE/OPERATIONS Continued

Objective: Create ability to meet Newscheme customer service requirements

KEY TASKS	PROGRAMMES	RESPONSIBILITY	DATE & COST	TARGET
Process incoming points debit and credit transactions, and account maintenance transactions				Ensure efficient treatment of incoming transactions
Monitor performance and remedy any service failures				Ensure best practices and maintain agreed operating standards

SYSTEMS

Objective: Provide scalable and effective IT infrastructure to support all operational, customer service, financial and business management requirements

KEY TASKS	PROGRAMMES	RESPONSIBILITY	DATE & COST	TARGET
Develop cardholder management system, including card issue				All to be confirmed
Develop merchant management system, including terminals			All built and tested	
Develop loyalty management system			L minus 5	
Develop financial and reporting system				
Develop website				

PURCHASING

Objective: Ensure redemption awards are provided which ensure continuing customer appeal and interest at prices which reflect programme's large and increasing buying power, and are fulfilled efficiently

KEY TASKS	PROGRAMMES	RESPONSIBILITY	DATE & COST	TARGET
Issue requests for proposals to potential providers, evaluate responses and appoint				Ensure timely, responsive provision of attractive and competitively Built and tested priced rewards
Build provider links to I/B customer calls, customer service centre, website and loyalty platform			L minus 5	Develop efficient infrastructure to support rewards ordering and fulfilment
Evaluate service and buying performance and correct as necessary				–Maintain agreed operating service standards –Maintain constant pressure to drive down cost of redeemed points

LEGAL

Objective: Ensure all contractual and other commitments are responsive to Acme's legal rights and obligations

KEY TASKS	PROGRAMMES	RESPONSIBILITY	DATE & COST	TARGET
Finalise purchase and service contracts (BankBusiness and NewCo) and shareholder agreements (NewCo only)				Ensure Acme's business and legal interests are protected
Develop Terms & Conditions (Collector contract)				Ensure Acme's business and legal interests are protected, while meeting any statutory requirements on e.g. data protection
Search and register brand trademarks				Protect chosen brand identity
Review all provider contracts				Ensure Acme's business and legal interests are protected

RISK STATEMENT

Risk factor	Possible consequences	Seriousness rating	Probability	Action plan
Failure to recruit key partner	Scheme significantly less attractive, hence low enrollment	High	Low: agreements in principle already obtained	Alternative candidates already identified for each major sector. If these fail to materialise by L minus 90, cancel launch
Major system failure failure at launch	Inability to process applications. Negative PR	High	Very low: higher volumes already successfully processed	Standby third party back-up already identified to deal with peak traffic re-routes; staff training in hand
Enrolments lower than forecast	Programme becomes unprofitable	High	Medium	Divert all marketing resources to recruitment. Reduce non-acquisition costs. Review at L plus 90

DRAFT EXIT STRATEGY

BACKGROUND

A time may come when market, performance or policy changes make it necessary for Acme to exit the Newscheme programme. By the same token, it is also necessary to consider the situation if one or more Core Partners decide the programme no longer meets their requirements.

In deciding an exit strategy, somewhat different considerations apply depending on whether the programme is being run by Acme (BankBusiness) or by NewCo (a new entity set up by the bank and its partners).

1. BANK EXITS BANKBUSINESS

1.1 Goal

To allow Acme to exit the Newscheme programme if it is clearly not meeting and has no reasonable chance of meeting its business targets. At the same time, to minimise adverse publicity and potential damage to Partner relationships.

1.2 Partner strategy

- The contract between the Partners and Acme must provide for Acme exiting the business, while at the same time offering the Partners a reasonably long time frame for what will be a significant marketing investment.

One possibility would be to set the contract time period for say five years, with an option to renew for a further five. At the same time, the agreement should make provision for annual performance review by Acme, with an associated option for it to terminate the programme 'for cause' each year from Year Two onwards.

1.3 Collector strategy

- The possibility of programme termination must also be written into the Collector Agreement.

The principle should be to terminate the programme as quickly as possible, while minimising adverse publicity. Consequently, while points issue can be halted fairly rapidly, reasonable time has to be allowed for points already accrued to be redeemed. The issue of points should be discontinued after a fixed date, possibly no more than four weeks after the termination announcement. Redemption of points may be terminated after a maximum of six months (merchandise only), perhaps stretching to a maximum of twelve months if a substantial proportion of flight redemptions is expected. It may be tempting to impose a shorter time period, but this could create capacity and customer service problems.

A public statement should be made along the following lines: 'The Newscheme Programme has performed very well over the past X years, but customer needs are in constant change, and we must now respond to that by focusing on other methods of generating customer value. (An example might be by introducing a new card product with a menu-driven pricing structure.) All collectors will be given a reasonable time (specify) in which to redeem their points.' This announcement should be made to all currently registered collectors, using a combination of DM, card statements, e-mail, website, call centre, PR announcements, and POS.

2. BANK EXITS NEWCO

2.1 Goal

To allow Acme to exit the Newscheme programme if it is clearly not meeting and has no reasonable chance of meeting its business targets. At the same time, to minimise adverse publicity and potential damage to Partner relationships.

2.2 Partner strategy

- The possibility of Acme exiting NewCo must be envisaged in the Shareholder Agreement.

It is possible that the other shareholders would wish to continue, with or without another banking partner; in fact, if an exit clause for Acme is incorporated in the NewCo agreement, they may well insist on such an option. Under these circumstances, arrangements would have to be made to:

- offer Acme's shareholding to the other Core Partners;
- secure for Acme an appropriate portion of the funds held in the Reserve;
- ensure that Acme had met any obligations it may have via NewCo to third party suppliers or others.

However, if all the shareholders agree with Acme to terminate the programme, then the need would be to:

- wind up the company, and settle any outstanding obligations it may have as between shareholders, and to third parties;
- after this process is completed and all outstanding redemption requests have been processed, divide up any funds remaining in the Reserve, probably according to shareholding.

2.3 Collector strategy

As 1.3 above.

3. ONE CORE PARTNER EXITS BANKBUSINESS

3.1 Goal

To minimise disruption and cost to the programme, reduce potential adverse publicity and retain flexibility in deciding a replacement.

3.2 Partner strategy

- Make provision for exit clause in the Partner Agreement before contract period (say five years for Core Partners) expires. Possibly set date for review three years after signature.

Exit should not be made easy, and definition of the conditions under which it might happen will need careful thought. An outline might be 'Partner shall have right to exit the programme before the end of this agreement, if Partner can demonstrate to other Core Partners that to continue with the programme would involve him in unacceptable costs or risks. If other Core Partners accept that Partner may exit, Partner will be responsible for meeting any outstanding obligations to other Partners, Acme and collectors, together with bearing all costs of exit, including but not limited to cost of systems changes and collector communication, over which last the remaining Core Partners shall have the right of approval. In the case of agreed exit, remaining Core Partners shall have the right to replace exiting Partner by any other organisation of their choice (or none), the exiting Partner having no right of veto.'

3.3 Consumer strategy

- Ensure that Acme reserves the right in the Collector Agreement to cancel, substitute or alter the participation of any issuing or redemption partner.

Announce any replacement as being an additional benefit over the previous offering.

4. ONE CORE PARTNER EXITS NEWCO

4.1 Goal

To minimise disruption and cost to the programme, reduce potential adverse publicity, and retain flexibility in deciding a replacement.

4.2 Partner strategy

- Similarly to BankBusiness approach, set contractual review periods at three and perhaps five years, using similar requirements to demonstrate need to exit, and obligations if exit is agreed.

Additionally, there should be a requirement on the exiting Partner to offer his shareholding to other Core Partners; if so, a decision will have to be taken when drawing up the agreement whether to establish a formula to fix the price, or whether to leave it to negotiation.

4.3 Collector strategy

As BankBusiness.

5. ALL (OR AN EFFECTIVE MAJORITY OF) PARTNERS EXIT BANKBUSINESS

5.1 Goal

To ensure an orderly exit from the programme, minimising costs and adverse publicity.

5.2 Partner strategy

- Just as the Core Partners agreed a model for setting up the business, so the Partner Agreement should foresee a method of winding it up.

Everything here would depend on whether Acme wanted to continue the Newscheme programme. If so, it would be necessary to implement the strategy above for one Core Partner, but apply it to them all. However, under this scenario, it is unlikely that Acme would want to continue the

Newscheme programme. The issue therefore becomes one of programme termination. The main challenges then are how the Core Partners will meet their obligations to each other, to Acme, and to collectors. A strategy similar to that set out under 3.2 above would probably meet the case of obligations to other Partners and Acme.

Lastly, Acme will also have entered into contracts with secondary partners and rewards providers. These contracts should provide for termination by Acme at its sole discretion.

5.3 Collector strategy

As 1.3.

6. ALL (OR AN EFFECTIVE MAJORITY OF) PARTNERS EXIT NEWCO

6.1 Goal

To ensure an orderly exit from the programme, minimising costs and adverse publicity.

6.2 Partner strategy

- The NewCo Agreement should foresee a method of winding it up.

The principles here will be very similar to BankBusiness, except that arrangements will have to be made to:

- – wind up the company, and settle any outstanding obligations it may have to shareholders and third parties;
- – after this process is completed and all outstanding redemption requests have been processed, divide up any funds remaining in the Reserve, probably according to shareholding.

6.3 Collector strategy

As 1.3.

In addition to these documents, the complete business plan should include:

- projected product profit and loss statements (and possibly balance sheet)
- projected cash flow statement
- customer service plan
- systems plan.

This would also be the appropriate place to include a SWOT analysis. Setting out the strengths, weaknesses, opportunities and threats faced by a project, this venerable planning tool still has value in helping managers to see the programme objectively. The table in Figure 9.2 sets out the main features and suggests a (partial) list of observations which might be made by a supermarket considering whether to offer a health insurance product for people over 50 years old.

Complementing the SWOT analysis should be a gap analysis: this simply is an audit comparing what the market currently offers with our best assessment of what customers actually need. Like most powerful planning tools, one of the most useful

Focus	Component	Factors	Examples
Internal	Strengths	Marketing Distribution	**Marketing** Potential customers rate our brand highly for service and value for money **Distribution** In-store customer service desks can generate qualified leads for telesales follow-up
	Weaknesses	Cost Skills	**Customer perceptions** We have never marketed this kind of product before, and have no established association with it **Cost** Our competitors will probabl... back-office costs, because ... overall volumes
External	Opportunities	Changes in: Population make up; lifestyle preferences; technology; potential partnerships; legislation; competitors	There are more older peopl... generally healthier and livin...
	Threats		Established insurers are kn... considering entering this ma...

Figure 9.2 SWOT analysis

capabilities of gap analysis that it can serve as a corrective to over-optimism: if no clear gap exists for what we intend to launch, then the product must stake its claim on superior performance or pricing or distribution or all three.

For instance, an audit of the market for travel insurance may reveal the situation illustrated in Figure 9.3.

Segment	Competing product(s) available?
Business	
Single trip	Yes
Multiple trips	Yes
Long stay	No
Leisure	
Single	Yes
Families	Yes
Multiple trips	Yes
Activity holidays	Yes
Backpackers	Yes
Elderly	No

Figure 9.3 An audit of the market for travel insurance

Clearly, a good deal will depend on the care taken with segmentation. Also, the mere existence of a market gap does not constitute a business opportunity: the segment may be too small to be worth pursuing, or difficult to reach. This is simply the starting point for the tasks of market sizing, detailed competitive analysis, product definition and so on which have already been considered. Nevertheless, gap analysis is always a worthwhile exercise. Nor is its application restricted to what competitors make available: the same concept can also be used to identify elements missing from our own product range, or as part of a strategic review to identify how we get from where we are to where we want to be.

SUMMING UP

To move management from initial approval to granting full authority to commit resources, a great deal has to be done: hypotheses need to be confirmed, research undertaken, models built and tested. To ensure that these all keep a sense of direction, it can be valuable to set up decision criteria; these provide a set of hurdles which, once satisfied, lead to the next stage. Usually, this process will call for a business plan to be developed: integrating all the elements and functions necessary to launch the product, the plan will also document the tasks to be undertaken to achieve this. SWOT and gap analysis will ensure that the business plan is properly grounded in the market context.

CHAPTER 10

The Launch

INTRODUCTION

Once the business plan has been approved by senior management, it is fatally easy to believe that all the thinking has been done, and all that remains is to put the plan into action. But not for nothing is this process often called 'execution': faulty implementation can destroy the most carefully developed strategy. The military have a phrase for it: 'No plan survives contact with the enemy.'

Painful experience has taught me the following lessons.

THINK IT THROUGH

The first major marketing assignment I ever had was to produce a substantial holiday brochure. As I soon discovered, this was a very big job indeed, and some months of hard work later, I was elated when the printers in Sweden rang to say that the first container lorry loaded with brochures had cleared Tilbury Customs and was en route to our offices in central London. At that point, someone asked where I had arranged for the truck to park while it was unloaded. In fact, it had never crossed my mind, not just to set up temporary parking arrangements – I had never thought how the brochures were to be unloaded, let alone where they were to be stored or how they were to be distributed. Very chastened, I had to ask for volunteers to move 34 tons of brochures from the truck and stack them in the corridors of the building.

MAKE SURE ALL THE INVOLVED PARTIES ARE CONSULTED

Mailing a corporate financial services product offering to the finance directors of all the international companies with operations in the Caribbean seemed to be a sure winner, and in fact, response levels came in higher than budget. The problem was that approval rates were much lower than expected. On investigation, it turned out that many multinationals were headquartered in the Caribbean for tax reasons, as a result of which they had very odd financial structures – odd enough for them to fall completely outside the parameters normally used for credit checking. As a result, our automated procedures were declining applications from some of the largest and most financially powerful companies in the world, on the grounds that they failed to meet our credit standards. Given notice, risk control could have arranged for these applications to be hand processed.

CHECK EVERYTHING

My toes also still curl at the recollection of a lavish dinner thrown for our most VIP business associates and their partners, the crowning moment of which was to be a half-hour cabaret specially commissioned from a very highly regarded TV comedy duo. The act – which no one had thought to check beforehand – was of unremitting obscenity. The best that could be said for the hugely expensive evening was that no one ever mentioned it again.

THERE'S LESS TIME THAN YOU THINK

Tell people as early as possible what the deadlines are, and why it's important for them to complete their tasks on time. This particularly applies where colleagues or outside experts are involved, such as lawyers to check copy, who are not familiar with marketing processes and schedules.

MAKE A PLAN – AND MAKE SURE IT'S REALISTIC

There is absolutely no substitute for planning. Launching a product is a complex activity, requiring the co-ordination of many internal and external resources. The table in Figure 10.1 is a partial list of organisations which may contribute in some way to the process.

Each of these bodies will have its own priorities, staffing problems, and internal procedures which need to be followed: failing to recognise these issues is courting disaster. Far better to seek their active involvement from the very beginning: that way, they are much more likely to work with you, and find solutions rather than problems.

As to how the plan is made, opinions differ: some managers are enthusiastic about using software such as Microsoft Project, while others prefer to use a wall chart. Either way, the need is for a method which compels careful consideration of timing and the interplay of interdependent activities, throws up potential conflicts, and allows progress to be checked easily.

CHOOSE THE RIGHT SPOKESPERSON

Every product needs a champion – someone who is its public face, and is responsible for its continued growth. Usually, that will be the marketing manager under whose aegis the product falls. At launch, however, it could well be desirable, for the purposes

External resources	Internal resources
Advertising agencies	Senior management
Media buyers	Regional managers
Design groups	Branch staff
Direct mail houses	Sales staff
Public relations agencies	Training
Printers	Human resources
Transport companies	Finance
Audio-visual production houses	Operations
Set builders	Legal affairs
Equipment rental companies	Public relations
Customs clearance agencies	Risk management
Launch venues	Systems
Travel agencies	Security
Hotels	

Figure 10.1 Planning the launch of a product

of gaining attention and demonstrating the product's importance, to have a senior manager take on, if only temporarily, the role of spokesperson.

In this case, there are four golden rules: make sure that your figurehead is:

- genuinely enthusiastic about the product;

- fully briefed so as to be able to handle questions about it with confidence (or know who to pass them to if not);

- comfortable and persuasive in front of an audience;

- clearing enough diary time to give the event their full attention.

Finally, but not least important, product launches are usually exciting: don't forget to enjoy yourself!

SUMMING UP

Once the business plan has been approved, the focus of the work changes dramatically from the theoretical to the practical. Launching even the simplest product or service will call for the co-operation and support of very many organisations and individuals, both inside and outside the company. Making sure that all these elements come together calls for the most scrupulous planning and double checking – all against a background of constant time pressure.

CHAPTER 11

Product Management Post-launch

INTRODUCTION

Usually, the reason for launching a new programme, or re-launching an existing one, is to increase profitability. As we have seen already, however, there may be other non-financial criteria. Whatever the goals that have been set, post-launch management should centre around the questions of:

- How are we doing?
- How can we do better?

The measures (metrics) for how well we are doing will clearly be derived from the product we are selling, and the reasons for setting up the programme in the first place. The same considerations, of product and objectives, will also shape strategies for improving performance. But whatever the context, managers of most financial services programmes are likely be concerned with the basics of:

- revenues
- customer acquisition costs
- activation
- usage
- retention.

For example, a European card issuer uses the matrix in Figure 11.1 to track key performance measures. Note that even this document does not capture account acquisition costs by channel, nor does it review how performance is changing over time.

How the portfolio is managed to maximise performance on these measures will depend on what overall approach is adopted: some organisations focus on a structure more or less based on the profit and loss account, while others are also adopting an account life cycle approach. Whichever is used – and a combination of the two makes most sense – this final chapter will look at typical measures of marketing programme performance and techniques for improvement.

Portfolio key measures snapshot

Product Label	Brand A consumer card				Brand B consumer card				Business card	
	Standard MasterCard	Gold MasterCard	Signia MasterCard	Platinum MasterCard	Gold MasterCard	Premier Visa	Classic Visa	Affinity MasterCard	Silver Visa	Gold Visa
Total cards										
Cards open										
Cards per account										
Active %										
Debit active %										
Average spend pa $										
Average transaction value $										
Revolve %										
Average balance revolved $										
Attrition % Voluntary										
Involuntary										
Charge off% Bad debt										
Fraud										

Active: at least one transaction in the last three months
Debit active: at least one debit transaction in the last three months

Figure 11.1   Matrix used to track key performance measures

THE P&L APPROACH

Whatever the product, it will or should have a P&L statement. This provides us with a logical and comprehensive way into assessing the programme's financial performance. Clearly, there are components of the P&L statement, especially in the area of costs – operating expense, for example – which will probably play an important role for any product, but which fall outside the influence of the marketing manager. Similarly, a proper understanding of the programme's well-being will include a review of non-monetary measures such as call centre performance on QA criteria; again, these are usually outside the marketing manager's control. Nevertheless, operating standards and customer service performance can have a strong effect on results for which the marketing group will certainly be held responsible – acquisition, usage and retention, for instance. It makes sense, therefore, to put in place mechanisms for reviewing what is being achieved at the various customer 'touch points', to ensure that, at the very least, you are aware of what is happening, and ideally have the ability to ask for performance to be improved if necessary.

By way of illustration, the P&L statement in Figure 11.2, which is based on the one given in Figure 6.1, page 66, has indicated those revenues and expenses which the marketing function will be expected to control. The choice of target groups solicited, for example, will have a direct bearing on amounts borrowed and account acquisition costs. There are others where marketing can have an important role to play with other groups in cutting costs: acquisition choices will influence the number of customers who prove to be poor credit risks and thereby increase the burden of bad debts.

REVENUES

In maximising programme profitability, marketers will probably think first about building business income. Diagrammatically, the options, which, of course, are not mutually exclusive – are presented in Figure 11.3.

Increasing product revenues – acquiring new customers

The most obvious way of building product income is to acquire new customers, and most of the discussion so far in this book has concentrated on this. But we should not be acquiring customers at any price: banks which fought hard in the late 1990s to build their corporate lending portfolios by competing aggressively on interest rates may well have built their loan books, but found that the rates they were charging (and the securities they were holding) were insufficient to support the increased risk of default when business took a down turn.

The goal for marketers today is to ensure that, from the whole universe of potential customers, we pick only those who are likely to be profitable.

But new customers are not the only way to build product revenues. Another option is to generate more income from existing customers. That is the subject of the next section.

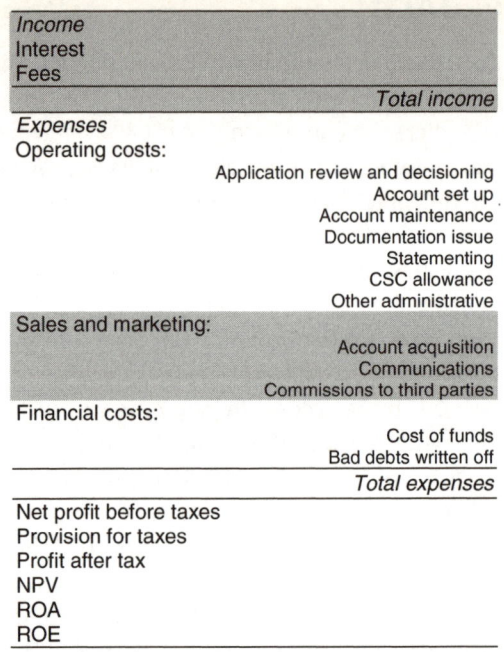

Income
Interest
Fees

                                                                    Total income

Expenses
Operating costs:

                        Application review and decisioning
                                        Account set up
                                    Account maintenance
                                    Documentation issue
                                          Statementing
                                         CSC allowance
                                    Other administrative

Sales and marketing:

                                    Account acquisition
                                        Communications
                            Commissions to third parties

Financial costs:

                                          Cost of funds
                                    Bad debts written off

                                                                  Total expenses

Net profit before taxes
Provision for taxes
Profit after tax
NPV
ROA
ROE

Figure 11.2   Profit and loss statement for the Acme Low Cost Personal Loan

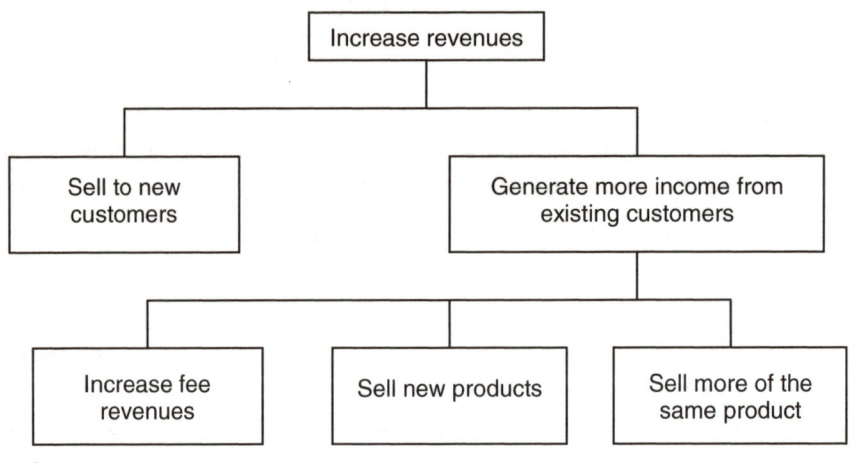

Figure 11.3   Building business income

Increasing product revenues – raising prices and setting fees

One straightforward way of increasing a product's revenues is to charge more for it. But there are limits to the ability to put prices up:

- *Competition*: In a competitive market place, if the product has no obvious and uncopiable advantages, our product's sales will fall over time, and a price rise may even result in total revenues dropping below their original level. If the market is less competitive, then what the economists call the price elasticity of demand will be lower (in other words, demand will fall by a lesser amount for a given price rise) and it may be possible to increase total revenues.

- *Legal constraints*: In many jurisdictions, the prices of financial products are under statutory review. For example, in a number of US states local insurance commissioners are responsible for overseeing and authorising premium levels. Rates of interest may similarly be under legal oversight.

Assuming that a price increase is legally allowed, great care would have to be taken to research customers' likely reactions to it. In a low inflation environment, typical of most of today's advanced economies, any price rise without a corresponding improvement in product content will be very problematic.

Accordingly, a much more frequent route to increasing revenues from a product is to see if there are any ways in which service fees can be charged. Figure 11.4 illustrates some possibilities.

Type of fee	Example
Fees for basic services	Mortgage account set-up fees; fees for account maintenance; fees for cheque processing
Fees for providing additional services	Membership charges for rewards programmes; ATM access fees; FX transaction fees
Fees for customer breaches	Over-limit fees; late payment fees; returned cheque fees

Figure 11.4 Charging service fees

In the US, payment card companies have been among the leaders in their zeal to generate fees: competitive pressures make it difficult to charge joining and annual account fees, and so these businesses seek to create income from customers who infringe the product's terms and conditions as shown in Figure 11.5.

Noteworthy here is the way in which most of the issuers vary the fees according to the perceived risk: the higher the balance, the greater the fee. Chase, however, takes a different perspective: its charges seem to be assessed according to the overall profitability of the customer.

It is not just credit card issuers who can exploit the possibilities of fees for increasing revenues: banks have also seen an increase in the income they generate from this source as shown in Figure 11.6.

Issuer	When applied	Fee
Discover	Balance over $1000	$35
	Balance less than $1000	$15
Household	Not reported	$35
Providian	Balance more than 2% over limit	$35
Fleet	Balance less than $500	$15
	Balance $500 to $1000	$29
	Balance more than $1000	$35
Chase	Non-preferred customers	$35
	Preferred customers	$29

Source: CardFlash, 3 March 2003

Figure 11.5 Over-limit fees charged by US card issuers

Fee income
(as a % of total income)

	Banks	Credit card issuers
1995	35%	18%
1996	36%	19%
1997	38%	21%
1998	41%	23%
1999	45%	24%
2000	49%	28%
2001	50%	31%

Source: R.K. Hammer Investment Bankers, quoted in CardFlash, 27 February 2002

Figure 11.6 Fee income

Figure 11.7, for instance, shows the fees charged by an Australian bank in June 2003 on a current account.

On the same theme, an article in the *Wall Street Journal* (25 April 2002) claims that 'Nearly 80 per cent of interest-paying accounts at Internet banks now charge service fees, up from 59 per cent a year ago, according to Bankrate.com, a consumer-finance website. The average minimum balance required to avoid such fees is $1239.10, up 49 per cent from a year ago.'

Nor are fees confined to retail banking: corporate borrowers are now facing utilisation fees when they take up part of an agreed credit line. Again according to the *Wall Street Journal,* Disney is paying a utilisation fee of 5 basis points (0.05 cents on the dollar) at 33 per cent line usage and 12.5 basis points at 66 per cent usage (*Wall Street Journal,* 2 May 2002).

Transaction type	Fee (Aus $)
Assisted withdrawals	2.00
ATM cash withdrawals	0.50
ATM transfers	0.30
EFTPOS	0.30
Self service phone	0.30
NetBank	0.30
Direct payments	0.30
Cheques written	1.00
Monthly account fee	5.00
Overdrawing approval	30.00

Figure 11.7   Fees charged on a current account by an Australian bank

But the most active fee-setters must surely be the US mutual fund industry, where investors pay management fees, administrative fees, custodian and transfer fees, shareholder-service fees, directors' fees, legal and audit fees, interest costs and marketing fees. These are in addition to fees for buying and redeeming shares in the fund (*The Economist*, 8 November 2003).

Perhaps surprisingly, there is evidence that customers do not necessarily resent fees: according to figures published by MORI Financial Services in 2003, the proportion of UK current account holders who have a packaged or fee-paying bank account had grown to 17 per cent (from 5 per cent in 1998), placing this type of account among the country's fastest-growing financial products.

Other key findings of the research were:

- Despite paying a fee, packaged account holders were more likely to be very satisfied with their account than those with a standard account (51 per cent against 47 per cent).

- Some 35 per cent of packaged account holders opened one because it was recommended to them, compared to 26 per cent of standard account holders. The key reason for no-frills account holders to open an account was 'because their parents banked there' (28 per cent). This reason for the selection of their primary bank applied, however, to only 15 per cent of packaged account holders.

- Packaged account holders were nearly twice as likely (17 per cent) to have made a purchase following the receipt of direct mail in the past 12 months, compared with 9 per cent of standard current account holders.

- Those with packaged accounts were also more likely (37 per cent) to have

found direct mail to be a useful source of information than their standard
account counterparts (32 per cent).
(*Wise Marketer*, 18 June 2003)

These somewhat counter-intuitive findings can possibly be explained on the basis
that customers prefer and are even prepared to pay extra for a product which really
meets their needs. When such a product lives up to their expectations, they are much
more willing to consider favourably service offers from the same provider. If this
hypothesis is correct, even in a competitive market fees can find a place.

Perhaps the last word on fee income should be left to a distinguished banker, Sr
Alfredo Saenz Abad, CEO of Santander Central Hispano, Spain's largest bank: 'In a
world of low interest rates…interest income will no longer be the main pointer for
performance. Revenues generated by fee-based products will be just as important'
(*Financial Times*, 27 January 2004).

There are alternatives to fees as a way of increasing product revenue. For
instance, lenders can alter the basis on which interest is charged: according to
CardData, grace periods on US credit cards have fallen by more than 28 per cent
between 1990 and 2002 as shown in Figure 11.8.

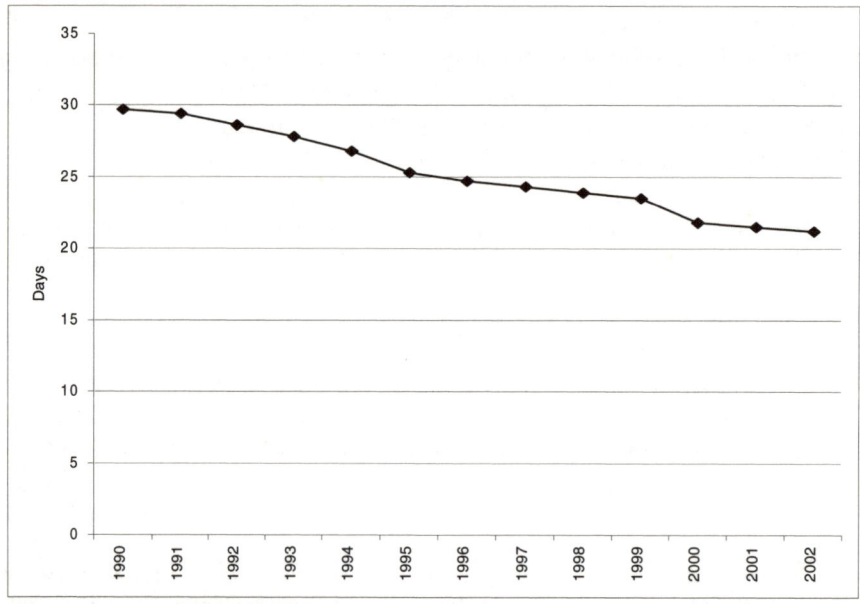

Visa, Mastercard, Discover, American Express
Source: *CardData*, 21 May 2002

Figure 11.8   Grace periods for US card issuers

Increasing product revenues – up-selling

Building revenues from prices and fees is not the only way to increase income: another option is to sell more of the same products to the customer. This could be as simple as, for example, encouraging an insurance policy holder to increase the sum assured, perhaps to reflect the impact of inflation or a growing family. Similarly, card marketers will seek to sell additional cards for family members to an existing cardholder. Again, in a business-to-business context, having once secured a foothold in a subsidiary, a bank may seek to extend its reach throughout a conglomerate.

A variation is to introduce an enhanced product, or one more in line with a customer's growing affluence. Thus, a retail bank will track its customers and offer a personal banking relationship to appropriate prospects. In the same way, a property insurer may introduce an upscale package with increased cover and sevice benefits. Of course, both will come with an increased fee. Generally, this process is known as up-selling.

Increasing product revenues – cross-selling

With many financial services products, the scope for up-selling is limited; few householders need more than one mortgage, for instance. But an existing mortgage account holder could well be in the market for payment protection insurance. This strategy, of selling additional products and services to existing customers, is usually called cross-selling.

Other examples include:

- the car insurer who mails customers with home insurance offers;

- the mortgage broker who (if qualified) offers mortgage protection or term assurance policies;

- the card issuer which markets unsecured loans;

- the bank which establishes a stock-broking service for its affluent customers;

- the accountancy firm which develops a specialised pension advisory service for its clients;

- the airline frequent flyer programme which markets offshore banking services to its top tier customers.

Given that the acquisition cost has already been incurred, most financial services institutions are setting targets for the number of additional products which they can sell to their customers.

Perhaps the most outstanding exponent of cross-selling in the UK is Saga: originally a hotelier which needed to fill empty rooms during the off-season and sold them to retired people, it became a tour operator specialising in holidays for the over 60s. Now, having seen the wider business potential of this increasingly affluent group of consumers, it has transformed itself into an extremely effective organisation for marketing financial services to them. Not only does it work hard at selling to its customers, it ensures that its products are carefully designed to meet their special needs.

Cross-selling and Up-selling

The opportunity
According to Tower Group, typical households in the US have 12 to 15 financial products supplied by five different institutions (*The Economist* 6 September 2003).

The aspiration
Wells Fargo wants each of its retail customers to have 8 of its products within the next two years, up from an average of 4.3 today (*ibid*).

The achievement
- The average Citibank customer has close to four different links to the bank. For example, one customer could have a checking account, a savings account and a mortgage.... sales of other products sold by Citigroup to the bank's customers account for 20 per cent of the consumer bank's revenues (*Wall Street Journal/New York Times* 18 February 2003).

- During 2002, Lloyds TSB achieved its target for each of its customers to have 2.5 products (*Press Association* 16 May 2003).

- Citigroup Inc. and J.P. Morgan Chase & Co. say they have started to receive more revenue than expenses from customer service centres. Citigroup estimates that it is bringing in 15% to 20% more revenue than expenses per month. American Express Co.'s cardholder centres also generate revenue by selling products to customers who call in, but the company's sales don't yet cover the cost of running the centres (*Dow Jones Newswires* 28 January 2003).

- Generali, Europe's fifth biggest insurer, sells its 30 million customers in Europe 1.4 products each, and believes it can do more. 'Successful bancassurers sell far more per customer' the company noted (*The Economist* 23 November 2002).

- Tesco sells only 1.2–1.3 financial services products per customer (*Financial Times* 30 October 2002).

- Only 50% of Abbey National customers buy more than one product (*The Economist* 1 March 2003).

- Intelligent Finance customers are said to be averaging 2.2 product cross-holdings, compared with the quoted industry average of 1.3 products (*Wise Marketer* 20 June 2003*).

Customer relationship management

However, for any of these strategies – recruiting new customers, upselling or cross-selling – to be effective, important preliminary work must be undertaken and the following are required:

- A comprehensive and up-to-date customer database which lists all the relationships which the customer has with us. In this context, it is sobering to see the findings of an analysis of North American utilities by Chartwell, Inc., which estimated that some 20 million accounts contain inaccurate contact details (*Wise Marketer*, 20 February 2003). Failure to keep the database current results in customers being offered products or services they already have, or ones that are not relevant to them.

- Fast access to the data, so that the customer record can be pulled up very quickly in response to an incoming call.

- Effective customer profiling so that product offers can be accurately targeted at those customers who past experience shows are most likely to respond to them.

- Carefully trained customer service agents who are capable of selling as well as responding effectively to customer queries and complaints.

- A remuneration programme which motivates the customer service team, without losing sight of the basic need to provide customer satisfaction service: 'Now, as much as 25 per cent of the (Citigroup) reps' pay is based on commissions they generate from sales to customers; prior to changing the centers, there was no commission-based component. Since the majority of a customer service rep's compensation is still based on customer satisfaction, the emphasis is on backing off rather than making a hard sell, say bank executives.'
  (*Dow Jones Newswires*, 28 January 2003)

Together, these components are known as customer relationship management (CRM), in which great hopes and even larger sums of money have been invested. The goal is to replace a plethora of product 'silos', each using its own, usually incompatible systems, with one single customer view, detailing all the customer's relationships with the institution. In its turn, this can be used to calculate customer profitability, improve customer satisfaction levels, and also provide opportunities for cross-selling and up-selling. Overall, the objective is to transform the organisation's viewpoint from being product-centred to, in the unfortunate current phrase, 'customer-centric'.

The goal is admirable; results so far have been patchy.

According to a 2002 Datamonitor survey, approximately 24 per cent of financial services institutions have seen a positive ROI on their investments in central customer databases, with almost 80 per cent of all respondents having invested in this component of a CRM system. However, almost 40 per cent of those surveyed say it is too soon to tell if an ROI can be realised from this investment (*Datamonitor Report No. dmfs1467*, 13 May 2002). A study by Gartner in 2003 reinforced the point: their research suggested that approximately 50 per cent of all CRM projects fail to meet executive management's expectations (*Wise Marketer*, 11 July 2003).

A case study from a US bank, however, shows what can be done:

> RBC Centura of Rocky Mount, North Carolina has 243 branch offices in the Carolinas and Virginia. It has created three classes of customers: A, B and C. Those in the A category are considered highly profitable and might qualify for lower rates on loans and credit cards. B customers are somewhat profitable; they can get fees waived on occasion. C customers, however, are barely profitable or cost the bank money,

---

A CRM Success Story

The UK-based telecommunications firm, BT Retail, expects to make cost saving of more than US$200 million by 2004, following its implementation of multi-channel e-business software.

In the firm's ambitious CRM implementation, involving more than 22 000 users, BT's retail division aims to achieve a single view of its 21 million domestic and business customers. 'BT Retail's goal is to create clear blue water between ourselves and the competition when it comes to customer satisfaction,' said Pierre Danon, CEO for BT Retail. 'Extending our channel reach, capacity, and capability will allow us to enhance the customer experience through improved choice, convenience, and responsiveness.'

Efficiency boost
By integrating a number of previously unconnected customer information systems, BT Retail will use software to optimise efficiency by migrating transactions to lower-cost channels, and by using the existing field sales force for the more complex deals.

BT is also rationalising over 100 call centres, and investing US$179.4 million in the creation of a network of 33 multi-functional, next-generation contact centres (comprising 31 in the UK and 2 in India), all of which will be powered by CRM applications.

This integrated customer understanding is what will allow BT to provide a more consistent, fast, and accurate response to the 850 million inbound customer enquiries received every year, whether through the Internet, telephones, mobile devices, field sales, or channel partners.

CRM savings
The new CRM programme is expected to save BT the equivalent of US$200 million or more by 2004. Already, overall customer satisfaction has increased by 3.5%, and customer dissatisfaction arising from call waiting time has been reduced from 28% to 2%. The total volume of calls needing to be transferred has also fallen by 27%.

Following the adoption of CRM applications, BT Retail has recorded a 10% increase in customer satisfaction among mid-market and large corporate customers and achieved a 70% increase in employee satisfaction.

And, thanks to the improvements in profiling and targeting, the company has also experienced a US$27 million incremental increase in revenues from its desk-based sales teams (*Wise Marketer* 13 June 2003).

which means they can expect more direct mail offers and sales calls as the bank tries to move them up to A or B status. For banks, profit measuring is new territory that requires the collection of more data on customers and their transactions. In December, NCR Corp., Dayton, Ohio, unveiled a software package – Teradata Value Analyzer – that can attach a dollar value to every customer, based on their accounts and transaction behavior. The bank can enter a person's name and find out how much that person made or lost for the bank over a given period. This past fall, RBC used the software to analyze the profitability of its 650 000 customers in the Carolinas and Virginia and found that it was losing money on 55 000 of them.

RBC branch managers called each of the 55 000, hoping to nudge them into increasing their business with the bank. 25 per cent added bank products or switched to accounts more profitable for the bank.
(*CRMDaily.com*, 22 March 2002)

The businesses which build and install CRM packages market them aggressively, and are understandably keener to talk about the successes of the approach than to dwell on its failures. But CRM is an enormously costly investment, and for it to work the whole of the organisation must adopt the same approach – not just in systems, but in every aspect of business management.

REDUCING ACQUISITION COSTS

So far, we have concentrated on portfolio management techniques aimed at building revenues. We now cross to the other side of the P&L account, to consider what opportunities there are to reduce expenses.

Apart from the cost of sales, there are few operational overheads which the marketing unit can directly influence. But within the sales expense category, profitable financial services businesses are obsessive about increasing the efficiency of their solicitation efforts.

Returning to the example given in a previous chapter, of the direct mail campaign featuring a consumer loan product, it is instructive to see the effect of improving the key variables shown in Figure 11.9.

Working from the base Case A, Case B improves both the response rate and the approval rate, to generate valuable cost reductions. Case C maintains these improvements, but also cuts the cost of the mailing, adding an equally worthwhile gain in performance. Taking all the changes together, the cost per approved application has been approximately halved.

In practice, it is rather easier to cut the cost of the mailing (by dropping elements or using lighter-weight paper to reduce print and postage costs) than it is to boost response and approval rates. Targeting segments with higher credit scores, for example, will probably help approval rates, but at the expense of numbers mailed, and may even

Mailing pieces	1 000 000	
Cost (including postage) per pack		$1.25
Total mailing cost		$1 250 000
Case A		
Response rate	0.80%	
Responses	8000	
Cost per response		*$156*
Approval rate	55%	
Approved applications	4400	
Cost per approved application		*$284*
Case B		
Response rate	1.00%	
Responses	10 000	
Cost per response		*$125*
Approval rate	60%	
Approved applications	6000	
Cost per approved application		*$208*
Case C		
Mailing pieces	1 000 000	
Cost (including postage) per pack	$1.00	
Total mailing cost	$1 000 000	
Response rate	1.00%	
Responses	10 000	
Cost per response		*$100*
Approval rate	60%	
Approved applications	6000	
Cost per approved application		*$167*

Figure 11.9   Improving the key variables

reduce response performance given the volume of communications aimed at these groups. Simply changing the score card to generate higher approval rates is fraught with danger, as it may well reduce account quality. In any event, it would be very unusual for marketing managers to have this authority, which would normally be vested with risk management. On the other hand, marketing should always work with credit control to ensure that the score cards and other tools being used to manage risk are not too conservative, declining potentially profitable business. Equally, diving too deep into the prospect pool is unwise: the constant challenge is to balance risk and reward.

Even modest improvements in acquisition performance can lead to very worthwhile savings. When the mailings are as large as those which for example Capital One routinely mounts, the dollar benefits can be spectacular.

This is where testing is so valuable: it can examine whether the inclusion of all the items in the pack is absolutely necessary, or whether it would perform just as well without one of the inserts. Apart from taking great care with the weight of the pack, so that it does not unnecessarily fall into a higher mailing cost bracket, good practice also dictates ensuring that all the mailing discounts offered by the postal authorities (for volume and pre-sorting, typically) have been exploited.

Mail Discounts

A three-year 'Negotiated Service Agreement' between the U.S. Postal Service and Capital One was approved yesterday by the Postal Rate Commission. Under terms of the proposed deal, Capital One will receive volume discounts between 3 cents and 6 cents per piece, depending on mail volume. The deal caps the discount at $40.6 million for the three year term. The proposed agreement also requires Capital One to receive address corrections electronically instead of having undeliverable mail returned. The deal, if approved, is unprecedented and will likely produce a number of similar deals for major direct mail users such as MBNA, Bank One, and Citibank.

The Capital One agreement still needs the approval of USPS Board of Governors which meets in early June. Reportedly, Capital One is the largest producer of first-class mail and the USPS' fourth-biggest customer. Capital One mails out more than 1.2 billion pieces of mail annually, and currently pays 29 cents for first-class mail. Industry wide, nearly five billion credit card solicitations were mailed in the USA last year, according to CardWatch.

CardFlash 21 May 2003

Nor should testing to reduce acquisition costs be confined to pack types and creative approaches. Lists and channels should also be compared, to ensure that we are acquiring customers as efficiently as possible. Profiling is a valuable tool here: by identifying the characteristics of profitable current customers, and then targeting solicitation activity at prospects with similar characteristics, acquisition costs can be cut and likely profitability improved.

The diagram in Figure 11.10 provides an outline of the main steps involved in creating a cost-effective list of potential solicitation prospects: the process involved is the same no matter whether the medium is post, telephone or e-mail, but can be considerably more elaborate than shown here.

THE ACCOUNT LIFE CYCLE MANAGEMENT APPROACH

The value of the life cycle concept is that it requires marketing activity to be determined by the stage (see Figure 11.11) each account is at, rather than treating the entire portfolio as if it were at the same point in its history.

ACQUISITION

To begin with, of course, we need an account to manage: this is the task of the acquisition process, which has been the theme of much of the discussion so far. Traditionally, once the sale had been made, the marketing task was largely felt to be over: one of the strengths of the life cycle management approach is that it focuses sharply on what happens afterwards.

Process	**Example**
Analyse sources of profit	• Interest income • Transaction fees • Low/no claims record
Identify profitable behaviour	• Maintain high credit balances • Good repayment history • High dealing frequency
Profile profitable customers	• High net worth individuals • Home owners over 30 • Older drivers
Identify prospects who meet profile	• Scan customer base • Buy in appropriate lists
Clean up list: internal screens	• Already own • Do not mail/Do not call • Fail internal risk criteria
Clean up list: external screens	• Low/no credit score • Do not mails/Do not calls • Addresses out of catchment area

Figure 11.10 Steps for creating a list of potential solicitation projects

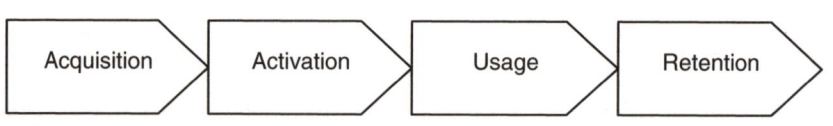

Figure 11.11 Account lifestyle stages

ACTIVATION

This is not an issue with every financial services product, but it is an important consideration with many of them. It refers to the situation where, for example, an investment account has been set up or a credit card has been issued, but the customer has failed to pay in funds, or use the card. Clearly, inactive new accounts have incurred all the costs of acquisition and set-up, but have failed to generate any corresponding revenues. They are therefore a dead loss to the business.

There is another type of inactivity: where an account, once fully used, becomes dormant. Here, although some revenue has been generated to offset the initial costs, there is a real risk to the customer's potential profitability.

The effect of inactive and dormant accounts can be seen in the matrix in Figure 11.12, which represents the experience of a European credit card issuer.

		Account age		
Payer type	*<1 yr*	*1–2 yrs*	*3–5 yrs*	*6+ yrs*
< 1 yr old	(54)			
Full repayer		(6)	2	0
Occasional borrower		26	54	54
Permanent borrower		50	113	152
Dormant		(22)	(27)	(22)

Account types	*% of portfolio*
Dormant accounts: 12+ months no debit or credit activity	5.4%
Full repayers: Interest paid up to twice in last 12 months	33.3%
Occasional borrowers: Interest paid 3–11 times in last 12 months	24.0%
Permanent borrowers: Interest paid every month in last 12 months	28.3%
<1yr: Accounts less than 1 yr old, not classified by behaviour	9.0%

Figure 11.12   Contribution to revenue by account type (Euros)

At one end of the spectrum, long-established permanent borrowers are by far the most profitable customers: this is only to be expected, as their initial acquisition and set-up costs have long since been recovered, while on the income side, they are generating interest revenue every month. By contrast, dormant accounts are the least profitable, as they carry all the initial start-up expense without producing any offsetting income.

Interesting and valuable though this exercise was for the bank which undertook it, it could still have been improved:

- Accounts less than 1 year old could have been analysed to trace the effect of inactives.

- A further segmentation of occasional borrowers into, say, interest paid 3–6 times and 7–11 times in the last 12 months may have thrown up interesting patterns.

- Most strikingly, 12 months is surely too long a period for an account to qualify as dormant: given the risk of loss (of potential revenue, if not necessarily real losses), it would be far better to have begun to track dormancy much earlier, defining it as no non-interest debit transactions for say three months.

Worst of all, dormant accounts can be defecting accounts in the making. Rather than let them get to the stage where the account has to be expensively retained, or re-solicited (see page 171) it is far better to treat dormancy as an early sign of a potentially attriting account. Spotting the signs early can save a lot of money.

One final note on inactive accounts: customers do die, and every care should be taken to ensure that deceased accountholders are not solicited.

USAGE

Having expensively recruited the customer and set up their account, it clearly makes sense to encourage as much use of it as possible.

As the following Figure 11.13 shows, seasonality – when the product is offered – can play an important role in stimulating usage.

Savings products	Lending products
Just before the tax year ends	Moving home
Just before Budget time	Christmas
Just after school fee payment time	Annual holidays
In the New Year	Just before school fee payment time

Figure 11.13 Seasonality in stimulating usage

Figure 11.14, for example, is a letter sent out by a credit card company when it receives notification of a change of address: recognising that moving home is a time when finances can be under pressure, it offers a convenience cheque chargeable against the card account.

However, there is an important rider to usage campaigns: they should be targeted only at good customers. Although 'good' will usually imply 'profitable', what constitutes 'good behaviour' will vary according to context. In a lending programme, it will be a borrower who meets his repayment commitments. In a savings

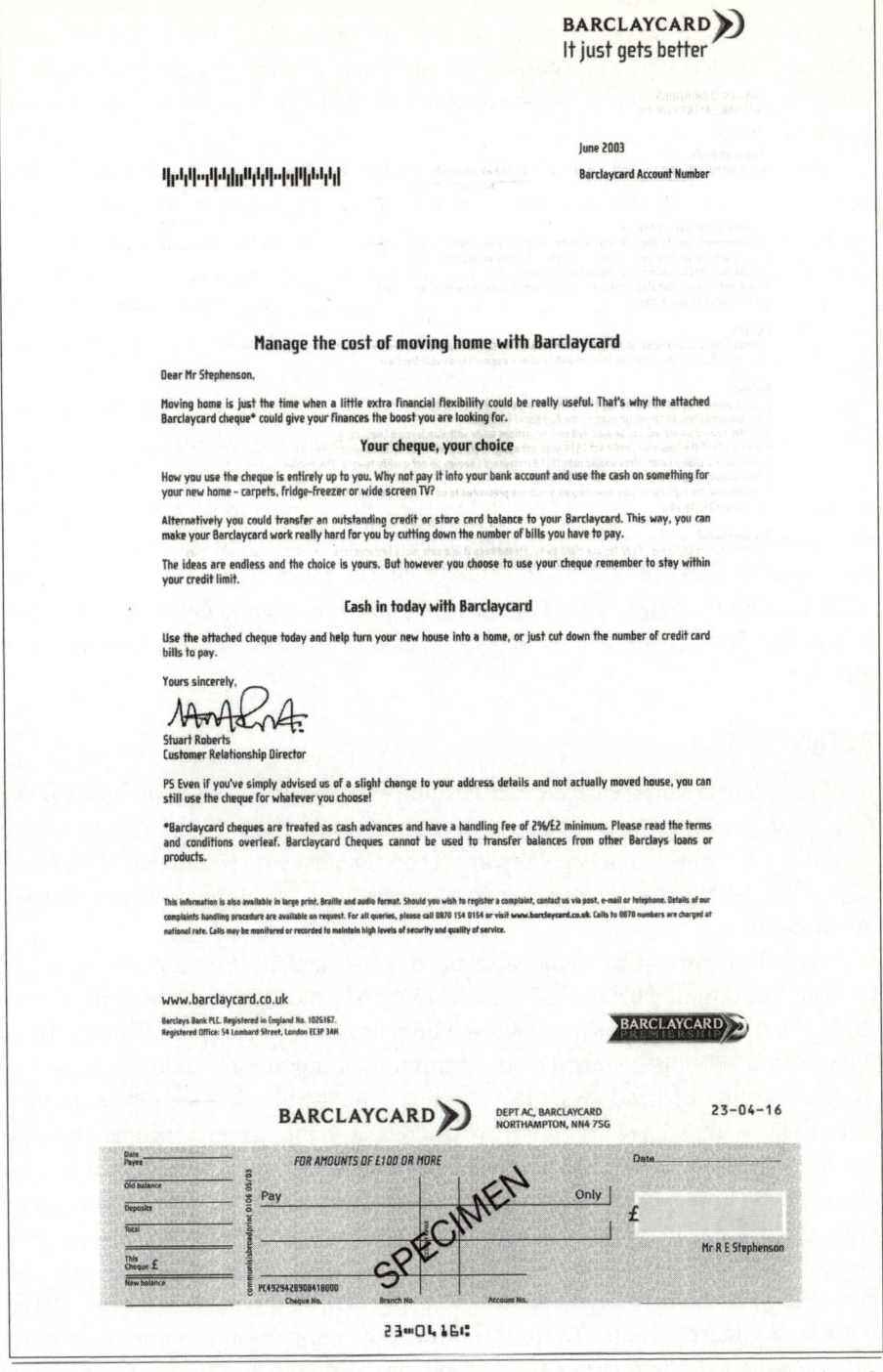

Figure 11.14 Usage letter prompted by address change notification. Reproduced with permission of Barclaycard

programme, a 'good' customer may be one who invests substantial sums and leaves them untouched over long periods. For a bank, it may be a client with a number of profitable relationships. But whatever the context, and however 'goodness' is defined, usage campaigns should be aimed very carefully at customers whose usage we want to see more of.

On the other hand, profitability can also be increased by negative usage campaigns: limits on activity levels, fees for excessive numbers of transactions, caps on amounts claimed, right through to withdrawal of facilities (where this is legal) all have a role to play in controlling unprofitable usage.

Line of credit management is a usage strategy particularly associated with lending products. This is a topic which arguably falls outside the marketer's domain, but which nevertheless is very much a part of portfolio management, and therefore merits at least a brief mention here. The point is that, if a borrower's line of credit is used up, he cannot borrow any more. This may also apply where his credit line is approaching exhaustion, because many customers will be unwilling to take the risk of a proposed transaction being declined by the lender. The opportunity is to increase profitable lending by raising credit lines. The problem is that bad credit risks as well as good risks run close to their credit limit. Great care needs to be taken therefore; but judicious line increases to qualified existing borrowers can generate higher usage, leading to increased profitability, improved customer satisfaction – and a lower risk of attrition.

RETENTION

If allowing an expensively recruited customer to become inactive is undesirable, letting one go over to the competition can be still worse. Whether it is a life insurance customer who cancels a policy, a savings account holder who withdraws all his funds or an entrepreneur who closes a share dealing account, a costly investment is walking out of the door.

Should everything be done to retain them? No: not all customers are worth keeping. The unprofitable ones – or, more accurately, those whose history shows that they are unlikely to become profitable – should be allowed to leave with our blessing. But the profitable ones we should do everything in our power to retain.

Here again, the need for a view of the customer which gives a picture of their profitability is underlined: without it, we could be working to keep accounts which we would be better off losing. Such a picture also allows us to calibrate how much we should invest in keeping the worthwhile customers – because inevitably some will be more profitable than others. But note that the concept of 'profitability' needs to be very carefully defined: do we mean profitable at product level or – in the case of a customer with whom we have a number of relationships – profitable at business level? If the latter, are we prepared to cross-subsidise one product with another, and under what conditions? These issues need to be very carefully explored, and responses agreed with all the interested parties.

But before we can even begin to develop a retention strategy, we have to consider why customers leave (or 'attrite' or 'defect') in the first place. Typically, it is for one of three reasons:

- to take advantage of a lower price (or more attractive ownership conditions) elsewhere
- a competing product does the job better
- the customer's need for the product ends.

Clearly, if we want to make some offer which we hope will persuade the customer to stay, we have to know which of these applies. Little can be done if the customer's circumstances change, and they no longer need the product, but if the reason for leaving is to take advantage of a competitor's lower price, or more effective product, then options do open up.

But the only way to find out why the customer is leaving is to ask. Implementing a strategy to identify attritors, and then their reasons for defection, will also have the important benefit of identifying an overall price or benefit weakness in the product, which will need to be corrected. In any case, attrition interviews are a useful source of competitive information. For this reason, many financial service institutions have set up dedicated retention units.

Once the reasons for defection are established, it is then possible to develop a range of counter-offers designed to persuade the customer to stay. These may take the form of:

- a reduction in price
- adding value for the same price
- meeting the competing offer (if financially and operationally possible).

The following schematics in Figures 11.15 and 11.16 outline possible approaches to the retention process. There are others; for example, account profitability could be assessed before the file is passed to the retention unit, so as to ensure that they deal only with the potentially most valuable cases. Equally, it is possible to establish a separate channel for phone-in cancellations, so that retention offers can be made at the most appropriate moment – and at the customer's cost if the call is not coming in on an 0800 number.

Some of the most refined approaches to dealing with defection are found in the mobile telecommunications industry, where the phenomenon is known as 'churn'. There, defecting customers are graded, not just on their profitability, but also how far they are locked in to an existing contract. Accordingly, a valuable customer who is threatening to cancel three months out from the end of his contract will only get a small inducement to stay. As the contract comes closer to expiry, the offers become increasingly more generous.

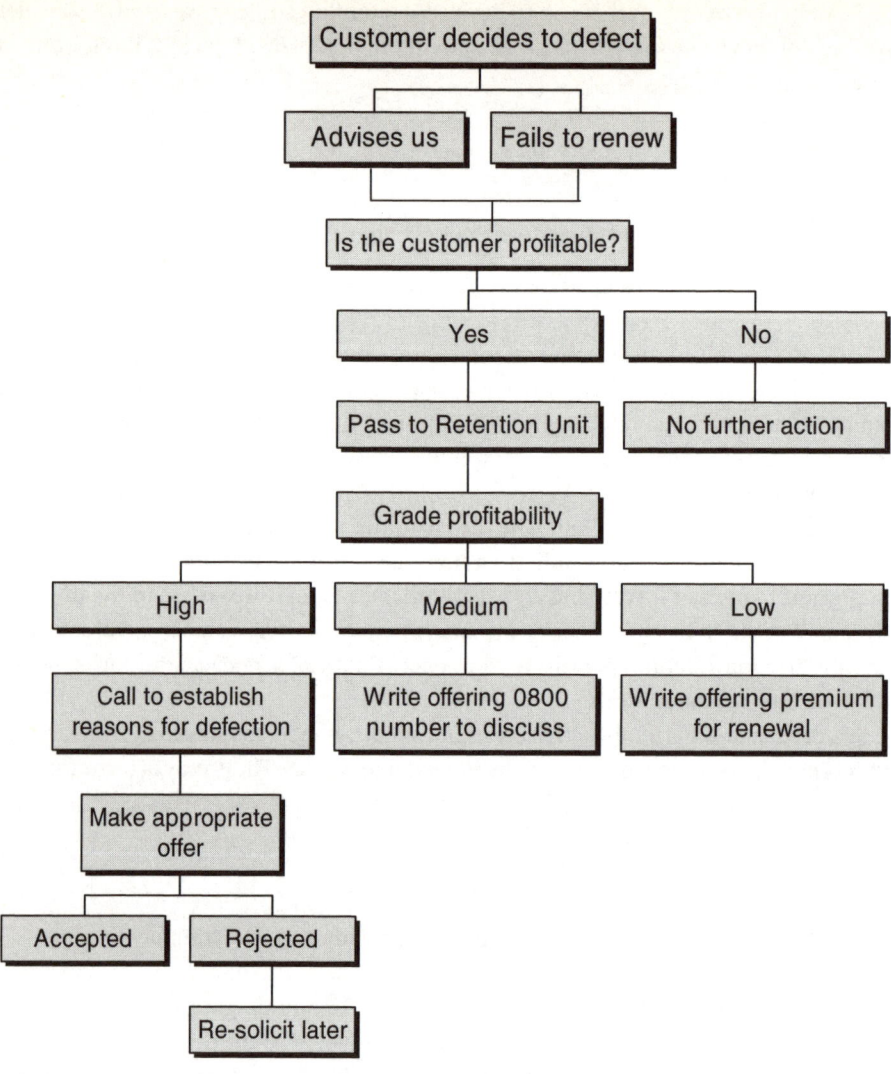

Figure 11.15   Retention process flow

Even better than cure is prevention – and some financial service institutions have analysed data on past defector behaviour to predict accounts at risk in the future. Examples of precursor behaviour include steady withdrawal of funds (savings accounts), paydown of balances owed without corresponding purchase debits (revolving balance loans), and sudden cessation of dealing activity (stock-broker accounts). Profitable customers exhibiting these behaviour patterns are contacted with offers directly related to a resumption of activity ('Keep your account balance over £1000 for 12 months, and win this clock radio') or simply a Thank You on an account anniversary or client birthday. One Brazilian bank sends its most valuable

The following matrix is being successfully used by a South American card issuer for profitable Gold Card customers who are threatening to cancel. The specific offer to be used is selected by the Retention Unit agent on the basis of the customer's comments, the account's profitability, and the cost of the offer. For example, a customer who said that she was cancelling because she no longer wanted to pay a fee for a card which she rarely used would be offered a downgrade to a free basic card. On this basis, the Unit is experiencing retention rates of around 20% (that is, it is retaining 20% of all profitable customers who announce their intention to cancel)

| | Profitability | | | |
	High	Medium	Low	Unprofitable
Offer selected on basis of customer comment	Upgrade to Platinum tier at no extra cost	Year's fee waiver	Downgrade to a no-cost no-frills card	
	Offer supplementary cards at no extra cost	Offer free payment protection/virus protection/extended warranty	Offer free card protection/virus protection	
	Year's fee waiver			Make no offer
	Bonus rewards points			
	Offer free rewards programme/card protection/ payment protection/virus protection/extended warranty			

Note, however, that even this large and sophisticated institution cannot take a whole customer view.

Figure 11.16 Customer retention offer matrix

customers a gift with a personally signed letter from the division president on their birthdays. Other institutions organise special shopping nights at favoured stores, or tickets to special concerts and sporting events.

CREATING LOYAL CUSTOMERS

Here, we are beginning to stray into the whole issue of how to build client loyalty. From being extremely fashionable, loyalty programmes are now going through a predictable eclipse in their fortunes. As usual with new fads in management strategy, their virtues were over-claimed, and their weaknesses are now correspondingly exaggerated. There is no space here to enter fully into the debate, but experience suggests that:

- Loyal clients can be unprofitable (think of the regular supermarket customer who buys only the specials), but the converse sometimes argued by revisionist academics (for example, Reinartz and Kumar, *Harvard Business Review*, July 2002), that disloyal customers can be just as profitable as loyal ones, is rarely true in the financial services industry, with its high acquisition costs.

- Loyalty programmes are not synonymous with rewards programmes: good quality customer service is just as powerful a creator of loyalty as airline miles.

- Too many rewards programmes have been launched on a me-too basis, without any attempt to set business goals, let alone a reliable way to measure performance against them. Much of the criticism comes from institutions who are the authors of their own misfortunes.

- Carefully designed and actively managed rewards programmes have an excellent track record at building incremental profitability through improved performance on acquisition, activation, usage and retention. The charts in Figure 11.17 set out how this works in the context of a credit card product.

Historically, banks in particular have relied on customer inertia as their main anti-attrition strategy. But there is growing evidence of the fundamental unsustainability in a dynamic, open market of the 'do nothing' approach indicated by:

- the entry of new competitors and new distribution channels;

**Payment Card
Rewards Programmes**

Getting it right

- Acquisition costs cut by up to 20% per approved account
- Spend up 60%
- Attrition rates cut by 20%
- ROIs in excess of 150%

Getting it wrong

- A financial services institution devoted 80% of its marketing budget to a rewards programme, but admitted having no idea whether programme performance had improved.

- A Latin American card issuer required four years' average spend for a cardholder to earn anything more than an entry level reward. The points expired in three years.

Rewards and the Life cycle

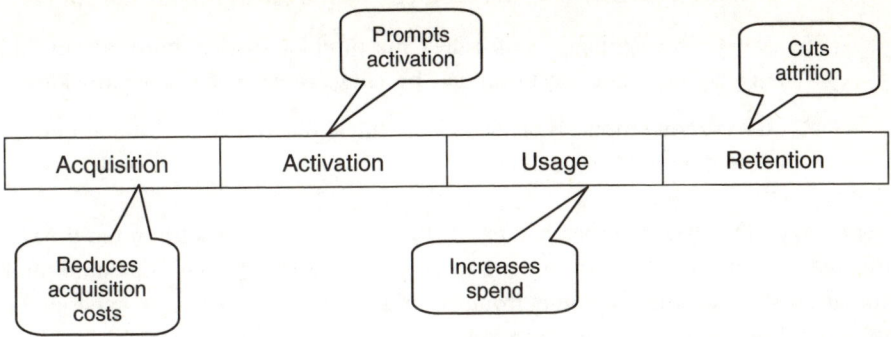

Designing a Rewards Programme
Sources of additional income

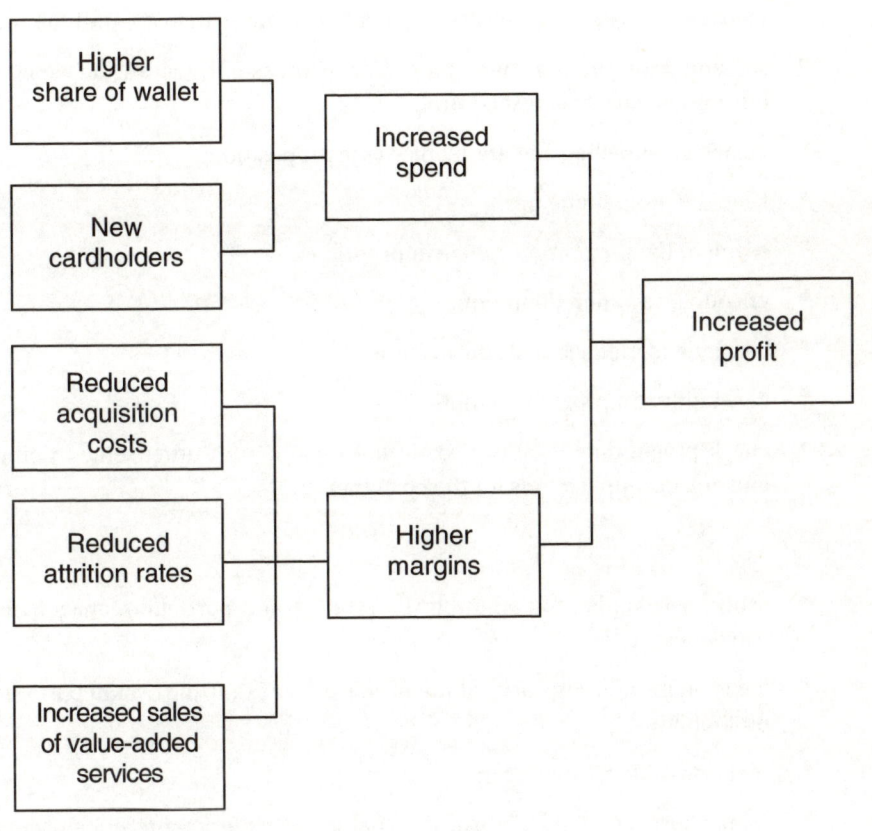

Figure 11.17 Effect of rewards on a credit card programme

- a much greater willingness among consumers to compare offers from competing financial services sources, even if finally they do not switch;

- 'cafeteria customers', who select the product most appropriate to their needs from what may ultimately be a large range of specialist providers;

- the current emphasis on cross-sell, which makes it all the more important to retain profitable customers.

Added to all this, recent research suggests that in Europe it costs up to ten times as much to recruit a new customer as to sell to an existing one. The same study concludes that declining customer loyalty is most acute in Spain, the UK and Italy, but relatively less troublesome in Germany, France and Benelux (*Customer Loyalty in European Banking, Datamonitor*, May 2003).

Following is a list of dos and don'ts when designing rewards programmes:

DO

- focus on changing long-term customer behaviour to increase profitability;

- set and monitor portfolio performance measures (activation, spend, attrition, revolve) against control;

- create a compelling and attainable value proposition;

- keep the programme fresh;

- segment the programme where appropriate;

- encourage award redemption;

- continue to manage costs downwards;

- constantly test programme initiatives;

- check programme legality, accounting treatment of unredeemed points and any tax implications for the customer.

DON'T

- expect a rewards programme to fix product and portfolio management deficiencies;

- focus on minimising costs, at the expense of maximising overall portfolio profitability;

- set impossible spend targets;

- think short term (in months): the goal is to create *long-term* behaviour changes (in years);

- make award redemption cumbersome: aim for points verification and redemption to be completed in one phone call (or e-mail);
- lose sight of the overall business objectives: improved response, activation, spend and attrition.

If, after all the attempts to predict profitable defectors and to retain them when they do attrite, the customers still leave, financial service institutions might take a leaf from the books of the best mail-order operators: re-solicit the most valuable attritors. Businesses which mail 'welcome back' packages to these accounts have experienced renewal rates of as high as 20 per cent.

THE ROLE OF RESEARCH

Research can be a valuable tool in portfolio management, particularly for hypothesis testing. Clearly, there is little point in research that produces information on which we can take no action: it may be interesting to know, for example, that a large majority of our customers believe that pension legislation is defective – but there is little we can directly do about that. On the other hand, if an equally large majority of our savings account customers say they are unaware of the pension products which we offer, then we might want to review our communications programmes.

The example in Figure 11.18 shows how planned research can examine the different stages of a decision tree, leading to conclusions which provide a basis for action.

PORTFOLIO MANAGEMENT IN PRACTICE

Maximising the profitability of a financial services product calls for action over many fronts. Successful portfolio management starts with approaching the task in an orderly and disciplined manner.

The first essential to bear in mind is, 'Why are we doing this?' If, as it normally will be, the answer is 'To build profitability', then a conceptual framework can be set up to make sure that no opportunity of reaching this goal is missed. The examples that follow are all based on the payment card industry, but the same approach can be applied to any financial product or service.

With reference to Figure 11.19, the goal is clearly to maximise the various revenue streams, and minimise the sources of expense. While most of the revenues fall within marketing's ability to influence (although actions affecting interest revenue will have to be managed in close consultation with risk control), only the cost of sales is fully within marketing's control. Nevertheless, marketing should have a point of view on such operational issues as cutting the cost of plastic issue by extending card validity periods. Figure 11.20 provides a portfolio management checklist based on these principles.

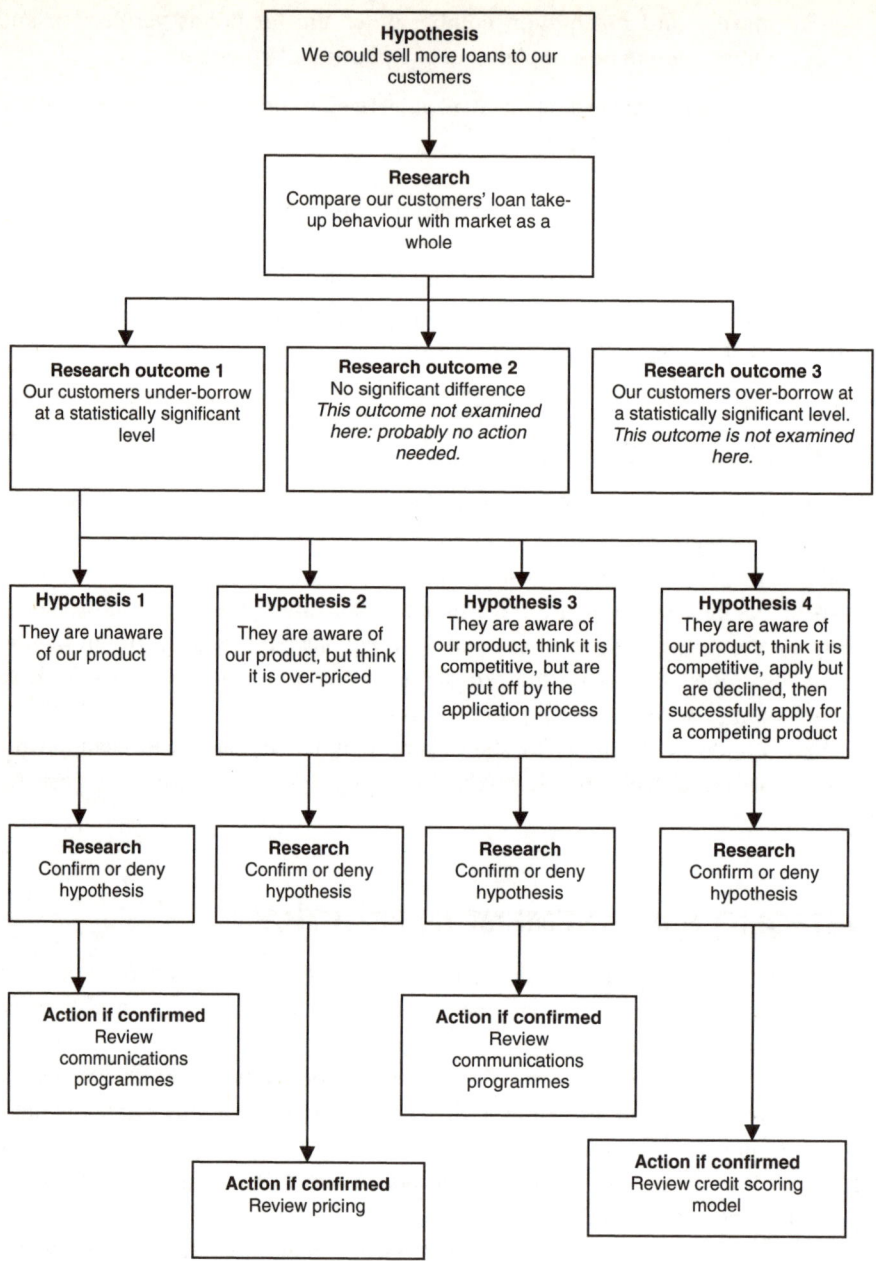

Figure 11.18   Using research to test hypotheses

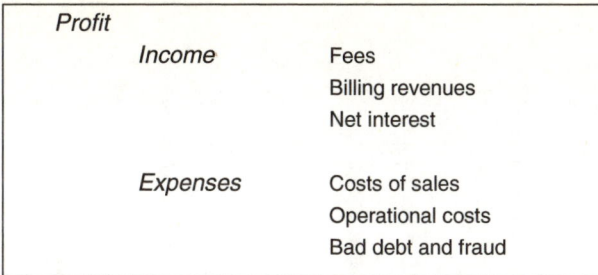

Profit

Income	Fees
	Billing revenues
	Net interest
Expenses	Costs of sales
	Operational costs
	Bad debt and fraud

Figure 11.19   Card programme P&L components on which marketing has a direct influence

The purpose of the account life cycle approach is to ensure that all the bases (acquisition, activation, usage and retention) are covered. Additionally, a 12-monthly time frame allows work to be phased over the marketing year, and also emphasises the need to ensure that work is carried out at the times of year best suited to it. For example, in many markets, customers are reluctant to buy new savings products around Christmas and New Year. On the other hand, travel insurance sales peak in early summer, as families plan their holidays. The chart in Figure 11.21 is based on managing a credit card portfolio, but the principle holds good for any financial services product.

THE POWER OF INFORMATION

Without good data, all decisions are guesses. With it, knowledge replaces shots in the dark. In the past decade, the availability of data, the power to store, process and analyse them has transformed the way in which marketing decisions are taken, as shown in Figure 11.22.

The point has been powerfully made by Sir John Bond, Executive Chairman of HSBC, when commenting on his bank's acquisition of Household International, best known for its sub-prime lending business. 'There are 150 PhDs at Household, who do nothing but try to predict…the actuarial likelihood of how people are going to behave. The technique is so sophisticated that they can predict how many loans will go sour within a 5 per cent margin of error' (*The Independent*, 11 August 2003).

Data Mining Defined

'An information extraction activity whose goal is to discover hidden facts contained in databases. Using a combination of machine learning, statistical analysis, modelling techniques and database technology, data mining finds patterns and subtle relationships in data and infers rules that allow the prediction of future results. Typical applications include market segmentation, customer profiling, fraud detection, evaluation of retail promotions, and credit risk analysis.' (*Twocrows.com*)

Personal card

Income

Fees

Component	Variables	Goal	Strategy suggestions
Annual	Fee level	Maximise pricing level	Monitor competition charges
			Understand cost base
	Number of plastics	Maximise sales	Careful list selection
			Train branches in prospecting and selling
			Establish 'Champion and Challenger' direct mail strategy
			Consider balance transfer offers
			Consider APR offers
			Consider annual fee waiver
			Maximise number of additional cards
			Monitor monthly
	Renewals	Minimise attrition	
		a: Voluntary attrition	Identify precursor behaviours and mail accordingly
			Consider profitability-related pricing
			Create retention strategy
			Create Welcome Back offers for profitable attritors
			Evaluate line of credit strategy*
		b: Involuntary attrition	Feed back into list selection criteria
Additional services	Number of services offered	Maximise take up	Research customer needs
			Establish 'Champion and Challenger' communications strategy
	Fee level	Maximise pricing level	Monitor competition
			Negotiate best deal with suppliers
	Renewals	Minimise non-renewals	Pre-anniversary mailings
			Create attractive offers for non-renewers
ATM	Availability to cardholders	Maximise no. of authorised cardholders	Feature in mailings
	Number of transactions		
FX	Charging regime	Affected by Euro billing	Feature in mailings
	Number of transactions	Maximise number	Consider in prospect targeting
			Consider in prospect targeting

	Interest*	To be considered with risk management	Maximise APR
	Late payment*		Maximise interest bearing balances
	Overlimit*		
			Establish with reference to competition and any legal constraints
			Feature in mailings
			Establish with reference to competition and any legal constraints
			Establish with reference to competition and any legal constraints
Billing	Billing volume	Number of transactions	Maximise number
			Offer insurance protection
			Build share of wallet
			Manage credit lines pro-actively*
		Average transaction value	Maximise value
			Promote high value T&E and business purchase usage
		Interchange %	Maximise average level
			Stimulate use in restaurants, hotels, high value retail etc.
Expenses			
Cost of sales	Cost per approved card	Number of applications	Maximise number
			Careful prospect targeting
			Train branches and manage performance
			Establish Champion and Challenger DM strategy
		Approval rate*	Maximise in light of risk
			Feed portfolio performance back into list selection
			Review score card performance regularly
Operational costs			Develop electronic MIS, billing and payment
			Consider extended card life
			Mail additional cards to client for distribution

Notes
* These aspects *must* be developed in consultation with Risk Management
Ignores financial costs - funding, debt management, and fraud

© Strategic Planning and Marketing 2000

Figure 11.20 Portfolio management checklist

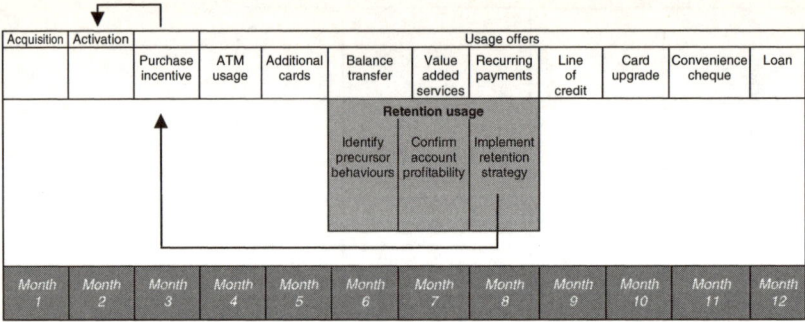

Figure 11.21   Managing an account life cycle: 12-month time frame

	Traditional	*Information-led*
Products	One size fits all	Targeted, segmented
Organisation	Hierarchical	Modelling and analysis-led
Objective	One product at a time	Maximise cross-sell
Management policy	Cautious – driven by risk reduction, not opportunity	Profitability driven, based on flexible pricing
Customer relationship	Static: defined by product held today	Dynamic: defined by potential product holding and profitability
Testing discipline	Minimal	Iterative, continuous testing
Measures	Maximise market share	Maximise NPV at account level
Tracking and analysis	Product level	Test cell level

Source: Adapted from Slawsky and Hall, 'Information Management', *European Card Review*

Figure 11.22   The changing approach to financial services marketing

The ability of data mining, as it has come to be known, to forecast at this level of accuracy transforms the nature of sub-prime lending: if the losses are predictable, then the risk is correspondingly low. Risk therefore becomes, not loans going delinquent, but loans going delinquent unexpectedly. Of course, the economic climate is in constant change, and the equations must therefore be re-calibrated continuously, but the power of the approach is undeniable.

Nor is data mining restricted to sub-prime segments or even to lending products. Its techniques can be used across the financial services industry and in every area of

---

Eagle Star Case Study

The need

In a price-sensitive market place, Eagle Star, along with all other insurance companies, finds that some customers defect and allow their existing policy to lapse.

Eagle Star was keen to identify those customers most likely to fail to renew their policies, allowing action to be taken before they switched to a competitor.

The solution

Eagle Star used sophisticated customer segmentation to understand the different customer types and predict which were most likely to allow their policy to lapse.

To identify the typical Eagle Star customer, marketers took a sample of purchasers for each product and segmented them into defined consumer groups, using individual factors such as age, lifestyle, shopping habits, newspaper readership and, importantly, income.

These customer profiles were then compared with the database of each product's buyers (e.g., pensions or motor insurance) to help predict their probable future purchasing habits. Customers that did not fit the profile were not contacted, reducing wasted time and resources.

The results

Eagle Star explained:

> Using sophisticated modelling tools and systems in our motor insurance division, we have already seen an improvement in customer retention of approximately 10%. We achieved this by building a model to predict which of our customers are likely to allow their insurance to lapse and then targeted those by telephone to talk them through the benefits of their insurance policy.

> We've achieved numerous benefits by using segmentation and profiling in this way. We have always tried to treat customers as individuals so, using these approaches, we can further improve our service.

> In addition, the cost savings on mailings and return on marketing activity have also been beneficial, and these benefits have even been extended to our brokers. By knowing the target audience, ads can be placed in publications that match the profile we have identified.

Eagle Star concluded, 'On the whole, it has given us an excellent return on our investment.'

Case studies reproduced with permission from Acxiom, UK

---

portfolio management: from assessing claim rates from a particular insurance mailing, through assessing the effect of fees on ATM usage, to evaluating the predictive ability of new credit score cards.

PRODUCT LED OR CUSTOMER LED?

It is hard to argue with the notion that marketing should begin and end with the customer. On the other hand, it is possible to lose the baby with the bathwater: product market share does influence profitability at account level if it generates

Co-operative Bank Case Study

The need
In a unique initiative, the Co-operative Bank introduced the UK's first Visa Gold Card guaranteed free of annual charges for life. The launch campaign, 'Free For Life', was divided between national press advertising and direct mail. In both cases accurate media and list selection was essential, not only to meet their recruitment targets but also to ensure that applicants met the bank's strict acceptance criteria.

The solution
The bank selected data from four databases for its launch campaign, including one based on lifestyle. The bank's reasons: 'Our target audience was well defined - income £25 000+ with an existing credit card. Lifestyle data was an obvious choice for direct mail because it offers such a broad range of demographic selections at individual level.'

The results
Lifestyle was the top performing database, achieving a response of 7%. The bank noted that 'The overall results from direct mail were often more cost-effective and the quality of response was higher than that received from press advertising.'

As a result, the bank extended its campaign with a 300 000 mailing utilising lifestyle data. Against a target of 12 000 responders, this generated 21 000 applicants and reduced the average cost per new customer by 35%.

Case studies reproduced with permission of Acxiom, UK

Bradford & Bingley Case Study

The need
Bradford & Bingley had the largest independent sales force of any UK building society. The Society wanted to promote its financial planning service and generate qualified leads for their branch network on a regular basis.

Off-the-page advertising had produced 0.6% response, but Bradford & Bingley were looking to achieve an improved cost per response for long-term lead generation.

The solution
The first step was to profile their existing customers using data to accurately define the target audience.

Key characteristics, including age 35–64, married, with known interest in personal finance, were used to select 40 000 prospects for direct mail from a lifestyle database. These were divided into 5 geographical groups to dovetail with Bradford & Bingley's regional network. The mail pack invited recipients to a free, no obligation, independent financial review at a time and place of their choice.

The results
Direct mail generated a response rate three times greater than off-the-page advertising including a response of over 6% for the Eastern region. Cost per lead was almost half that anticipated, establishing direct mail as a cost-effective medium for lead generation.

To refine the targeting for a continuation test, project managers profiled responders and then adjusted the selection criteria to extract a more wealthy and upmarket target audience for a 20 000 follow on campaign.

Case studies reproduced with permission of Acxiom, UK

volume-led economies of scale, or if it is sufficiently commanding for competitors to quit the market. Again, abandoning calculations of profitability at product level will almost certainly lead sooner or later to distortions in resource allocation. Recognising the deficiencies of product-led management ought not to lead to losing those elements of it that are valuable. In fact, there is every reason to combine the best of both approaches.

SUMMING UP

Although product launch is perhaps the most exhilarating marketing assignment, it is usually how the product is managed afterwards which determines its long-term profitability.

Whatever measures are used to check performance, the key requirements in portfolio management are to be:

- structured

- comprehensive

- orderly.

The overall approach can be based on the profit and loss account (maximise revenues, minimise those costs which fall within our remit), or more broadly on account life cycle (manage marketing activities on each account according to which life stage it is at – acquisition, activation, usage or retention). Nor need these two approaches be mutually exclusive: in fact, the account life cycle concept is simply a way of delivering performance improvements which will almost certainly have measurable financial outcomes.

Data mining has hugely expanded the options in portfolio management: thanks to IT developments which have made it much cheaper to store information and faster to manipulate it, marketers can now build comprehensive histories of their customers' transaction history. By combining this data with personal information about their income and lifestyle, powerful statistical techniques can be used to predict where similar new customers could be found and what additional products existing customers could be sold.

Ultimately, portfolio management at its best is able to give confident answers to the following questions:

- What is profitable behaviour?

- Can we identify those customers who behave profitably today?

- Can we identify those customers who might behave profitably tomorrow?

- How might we stimulate that behaviour?

The power of this approach is that, once we know who our (actually and potentially) profitable customers are, we can then begin to profile them: this profile then serves as the best possible indicator of which target groups to solicit – which starts the whole marketing cycle again.

Index

If you have found this book useful you may be interested in other titles from Gower

Credit Management Handbook 5ed
Burt Edwards
0 566 08585 2

Handbook of Financial Planning and Control 3ed
edited by Robert P. Greenwood
0 566 08372 8

Handbook of International Credit Management 3ed
Brian W. Clarke
0 566 08376 0

Activity Based Management:
Improving Processes and Profitability
Brian Plowman
0 566 08145 8

The Gower Handbook of Management 4ed
edited by Dennis Lock
0 566 07938 0

Statistical Sampling and Risk Analysis in Auditing
Peter Jones
0 566 08080 X

For further information on these and all our titles visit
our website – **www.gowerpub.com**
All online orders receive a discount

GOWER

Join our e-mail newsletter

Gower is widely recognized as one of the world's leading publishers on management and business practice. Its programmes range from 1000-page handbooks through practical manuals to popular paperbacks. These cover all the main functions of management: human resource development, sales and marketing, project management, finance, etc. Gower also produces training videos and activities manuals on a wide range of management skills.

As our list is constantly developing you may find it difficult to keep abreast of new titles. With this in mind we offer a free e-mail news service, approximately once every two months, which provides a brief overview of the most recent titles and links into our catalogue, should you wish to read more or see sample pages.

To sign up to this service, send your request via e-mail to info@gowerpub.com. Please put your e-mail address in the body of the e-mail as confirmation of your agreement to receive information in this way.

GOWER